The Citadel
2024

"Making Art Makes Us Human"

The Community of Los Angeles City College

Featuring the work of LACC students, faculty, and the surrounding community.

Cover art: "Inevitable: Family, Friends, Lovers, Strangers"
Stoneware, Rope, 2024

by Jaice Metherall

Published By

The Citadel Board of Directors – Professor Jieeun Amanat-Lee, Professor John Lynch, Professor Sara Mortimer-Boyd, Professor Jeffrey Nishimura, Dr. Genevieve Patthey, Professor Kirk Sever, and Dr. Wendy Witherspoon

www.lacc.edu/academics/pathways/lhc/english-esl-dept/the-citadel

Editors: Jieeun Amanat-Lee, Matt Bernstein, John Lynch, Sara Mortimer-Boyd, Kirk Sever, Wendy Witherspoon

Editor-in-Chief: Genevieve Patthey

The work within these pages is representative of the voices of Los Angeles City College, but the writers' words are their own and are, therefore, not officially endorsed by the college itself, or the Los Angeles Community College District.

First Edition: November 2024

This edition was made possible by the generous support of the Los Angeles City College Foundation.
http://www.laccfoundation.org/

ISBN: 9798342015899

Stories & Poems

about how

Making Art

Makes Us

Human

"In Another Lifetime"
(Stoneware, Rope, 2024)
by Jaice Metherall

Table of Contents

Art: "In Another Lifetime" by Jaice Metherall   4

Editor's Note   8

Art: "Self-Portrait" by Nhayeli Sanchez   14

Stories & Poems about
"Making Art Makes Us Human"

"The Stump" by M. Isabell Cardenas   15

"Blues for Potato Jones" by Sally Hawkridge   18

"The Broken Hearts Club of Lieutenant MacLean"
by Igor Kholodenko   27

"Los Angeles" by Sarah Magnuson   48

"I Am a Rock" by Edna O'Brien   58

"Crown Vic" by Devin Olson   65

"The Final Application" by Tvisi Ravi   75

"Catching Shadows" by Liz Ogaz Ruiz   86

"Roadkill" by Aisani Washington   94

Art: "Pilgerflashe—Marine Style Vase from
Palaikastro" by Olaf Tausch   98

"Carpinteria" by Tyler Becker   99

"Pyrite Laureate" by Karine Beltran   101

"Poppy" by Isabell Cardenas   105

"Picture" by LuvLeighAn Clark   106

"Appetite" & "Starbuskers" by Kathryn Jordan   108

"The Roses Are Blooming" by Jessica Nayeli   110

"Absurdity of Inevitability" by Jonah Lee   114

"Period II Test" by Gilaine Fiezmont   115

Art: "The Flying Dove" by Yinghui Huang   118

Stories, Poems, & Essays from
LACC's 24th Annual Writing Contest

"Slaying Byron" by Emma Baker   120

"Yeshua & Yeast" by Rhyan Rose Kirsch   123

"Little Armenia" by Alina Melikian   125

"In My Solitude" by Lindsay O'Brien   137

"Fast Ice" by Devin Olson   141

"Here" by Erika Alexandra Ramirez   148

"Poem to My Favorite Person"
        by Alexandra Figueroa Cuellar   156

"A Christmas Toy" by Margarita Ismusova   159

"A Female Buddhist" by Hahn Kim   161

Authors & Artists   178

Special Thanks   187

Editor's Note

About two decades ago, University of Cambridge scholar Dr. Nigel Spivey proposed that "Art Made the World" in a series that explored human creativity going back 100,000 years and spanning five continents. Catching the series on my local PBS station, I found my grand narrative of human evolution completely upended in a most delightful way: No longer did human societies evolve in response to economic imperatives. Instead, it was their need to make art and celebrate community in the face of death that sowed the seeds for civilization. That need led to the creation of Gobekli Tepe—proposed as the world's earliest temple by archeologist Klaus Schmidt—on the hills of southeast Turkey some 11,000 years ago. What may be the earliest human monumental architecture brims with images of scary creatures like scorpions and vultures on huge megaliths and stone pillars.[1] Art turns out to be as critical to human survival as food and shelter, so crucial in fact that we may be 'hardwired' to create, to engage in symbolic imagery, singing and storytelling, and in collective performances.

Gobekli Tepe Archeological Site

Photographer: Recep Tayyip Çelik

The Citadel's 2024 edition is dedicated to that contention, with stories, poems, and essays reflecting on our human need to make art. And as with prior years, these reflections come from students, faculty, English language learners in our ESL program, and guest contributors who took up the challenge to consider how making art makes us human. We also feature winning stories and poems from the Department of English & ESL's 24th Writing Contest.

The Citadel has been published at Los Angeles City College since the 1960s, originally sponsored by Emeritus English Professor Sam Eisenstein. With support from the LACC Foundation, we endeavor to provide a voice to our students and larger community, a place to share diverse insights and thoughtful reflections about our shared human condition.

Every year, we are indebted to Visual and Media Arts colleague Alexandra Wiesenfeld, her colleagues, and her students for memorable visual art. Cover artist Jaice Metherall's stoneware installation "Inevitable: Family, Friends, Lovers, Strangers" takes us back to earlier art like the bulls gracing Lascaux Cave in France 20,000 years ago[2] and reappearing across Anatolia and the Eastern Mediterranean—including Gobekli Tepe—ten millennia later. Continuing archeological discoveries from times before writing reveal that we did not make jugs or baskets or shelters for purely utilitarian reasons; we made them artfully. A big thank you to all the artists who contributed their work.

As in prior years, the Citadel's Board of Directors has provided steadfast support and hours of volunteer labor as editors for our 2024 issue. A big thank you to my fellow Board members Jieeun Amanat-Lee, Sara Mortimer-Boyd, Jeffrey Nishimura, John Lynch, Kirk Sever, and Wendy Witherspoon, and to Matt Bernstein for continuing as one of our poetry judges. Thank you all for your ongoing commitment. There is no question that the 2024 issue would never have come together but for your dedicated and incalculable support.

In addition, *The Citadel* remains indebted to Professor Flavia Tamayo. Her work heading and coordinating LACC's 24th Writing Contest added nine wonderful poems and stories to 2024's issue.

A final thank you goes to the LACC Foundation and its Basic Educational Skills Trust for ongoing material support for our creative enterprise. Even a volunteer-led effort requires some funding, and the LACC Foundation has been steadfast in providing it.

In closing, we thank you for taking the time to browse the fruits of our labor and to read our stories. We hope our tales of survival and endurance resonate, and hope we can count on your continued support in the future.

Gratefully,

Genevieve Patthey

Editor-in-Chief

[1] Andrew Curry, "Gobekli Tepe: The World's First Temple?", Smithsonian Magazine, Nov 2008, www.smithsonianmag.com/history/gobekli-tepe-the-worlds-first-temple-83613665

[2] Luiz Oosterbeek in collaboration with Noël Coye, Conservateur du patrimoine, Ministère de la Culture et de la Communication, France, The Bradshaw Foundation, n d, www.bradshawfoundation.com/lascaux/

"Self-Portrait"
(2024)
By Nhayely Sanchez

The Stump

By M. Isabell Cardenas

First, they came for my surroundings, then for my neighbors. They tried coming for me but all they got were my limbs. They gave up and let me keep my trunk for a while, but eventually took that after a few tries. Now all that's left is me, the Stump.

My roots run deep around here. I'm not going anywhere.

I got here by accident. I don't remember how I got here, but an accident seems most likely. I sprouted along with my fellow trees. The taller I grew, the more I could see. A river around the way, meadows, and mountains in the distance. That's been the surroundings for centuries. Fires have roared and then rains came to replenish it all. Over and over. Loss was inevitable, winds taking some neighbors but something new always growing once again. You'd think things wouldn't change but they do.

Humans speaking Spanish passed by us. Marveling at the scenery. Taking and taking from us. Taking down some neighbors, slowly, to build churches, homes, and to keep them warm. As time went on more came. Speaking English and sometimes other things. As time went on, more was taken from us. The mountains in the distance covered with bold white letters. Some of my friends were taken down in order for concrete to be poured, making room for vehicles. Noisy with disgusting smells. The river, no longer a free flow, covered with the same concrete.

As time goes on the worse it seems to get. Foreign trees that soar into the sky with strange gigantic leaves planted by us. A palm tree. Rows and rows of them for miles. They don't look like they match here. But the humans seem to marvel at them. They love being admired. Soon after, perfect round trees were planted into the ground. But they are not alive. I cannot feel their roots. They don't have any. They just hang around, dead. But they have a job to do. To hold wires in the air that carry electricity for the humans. Because of the electricity I can no longer see the stars in the night sky. I miss the stars. One windy day, the palm tree's leaves fell on the wires and caused a fire. It burned all around and finally it reached me. I burned a little. And once the fire was done, the humans came to me and said, "We better take the limbs."

And they took more than just the burned parts of me. I was left bare with only my trunk. It was a struggle to grow. And the humans came once again and said they would be taking me down. But I persisted. I was stubborn and I did not move. So they took my trunk and left me a stump. They poured concrete around me and left me in a perfect square. This little square was all I had left to myself.

They tried to take me out a couple times. All of them embarrassing for the humans. Ha. My roots are too deep and if I go I am taking everything around down with me.

They left me alone for a while. I lived in peace for a while. If you call being used as an ash tray and dog urinal, peace, then yeah that was peace. But I figured a day would come. These humans always want more more more.

Men with orange plastic hats came to look at me.

"And when we rip this stump out, we'll be able to pave the ground for the apartment complex's parking lot."

"Is this the stubborn one?"

"This is oak #88. Yeah the roots run far to the left so it might take down some poles."

"Shit."

I can hear the beeps of the excavator coming towards me. They dug deep around and put a chain around me. The dead trees shook. I have roots around them. The humans got scared and finally decided to slice me from my roots. Up into the air I went. I'm the last of what used to be. And I will be no more.

Blues for Potato Jones

By Sally Hawkridge

Dominic Fillmore placed the tiny microphone on the battered TV tray table between himself and a man whose face was as old as time, so old that perhaps it had hit its limit, bounced back, and was getting younger because the oldness had no place else to go.

"Uh, testing, one, two..."

"That's a microphone?" The old man was incredulous. "Why, that's a microphone for hummingbirds!" A rheumy laugh exploded out of him. "For bugs. For a cockroach. Not even a big one. A little baby one."

He laughed and wheezed harder. Dom handed him a glass of water, which he refused because he had been laughing and wheezing for a good minute.

"Are you good?" asked Dom.

"Oh, I'm good!"

"May I start recording?"

"I thought you had been recording! You recording now?" He leaned into the microphone until his weathered lips nearly touched it and said in his deepest voice, "Let the record reflect, Your Honor, a microphone for ants and other insectoid forms of life." He sat up again and tried to drink water while laughing, spilling a fair bit down his front in the process.

"Dominic Fillmore, today is May 18th of two thousand twenty four. Speaking with Marcus Aurelius Jones Junior—"

"Potato Jones. They call me Potato Jones. Let the record reflect."

"Sir—Mr. Jones—"

"Potato!" thundered Potato Jones.

Dominc paused, stricken.

"Potato. Not to be confused with Potahto, a different variety of fruit."

Dominic studied his face until he was sure that the man's stern expression was in jest.

"Mr. Potato Jones, sir, um, do I have your permission to record this interview?"

"Well, yes, son, I invited you into my palatial establishment, didn't I?"

"Yes, sir—"

"Potato. Do not forget—" he waggled his finger—
"That I am a potato, a spud of the highest quality."

"Mr. Potato, could you please tell me how your first
recording, 'Blues for Rayford,' came about?"

"Do you even know why I got the name Potato?"

"No, sir."

"Because when I was a baby, my momma said that
holding me was like holding a sack of potatoes, with each
potato going in a different direction. I was small but solid.
Restless. I was always trying to go to ten places at once.
Not even one year old, and I was trying to go on a tour.
Everybody thinks it's because we were sharecropping
potatoes. Nope, we were growing tobacco, sugar, anything
that people get addicted to legally, plus rice and beans and
vegetables for our table. Wanna know what my first job
was?"

"Farming?""

"Hunting snakes." Potato Jones leaned in. "I was all
of four years old. My job was to find snakes so they
wouldn't get bit when people went into the fields."

"You were four?"

"I had a knife this long." He laughed at Dominic's
incredulity. "I bet your momma didn't let you have a knife
until you graduated high school. In those days, kids were
built different out of the country. We got stung and bit and

cut and every which thing. Just daily life. Things are different now. You know what I learned about snakes?"

"What?"

"Your rattler? It's the most just of reptiles because they warn you before they bite. If you respect them, then nothing bad happens. You have to have respect. That's why they have them churches around here where the people handle snakes. That's because people need to remind themselves of death. You need to respect the Lord because death can take you at any time.

"Now, there was one unjust rattler in the world, and that's the one that bit me without saying nothing. But even that one was just, the most just of all. You want to know why? Because I owe my career, fame, three wives, children, grandchildren, houses, and cars all to that snake.

"I was 11, running around like a raccoon, poking into everything I shouldn't have, skipping school, just running here, running there. I couldn't stand to sit still for one sweet minute.

"One night, I was sneaking around Old Zucker's farm. I knew that he kept some homemade hard cider under the porch where his wife wouldn't go find it. Would you believe, I came by his place every night for one month, getting closer and closer. I brought biscuits for the dogs to make friends with them, and after a month, I knew what was going on there, and when it was better than he did, I finally managed to sneak up to that porch. Now, Zucker was white, so you can imagine how that could have turned out. I guess I owe the snake that, too. He most likely saved my life.⬜

"So what happened was, I saw the glass of the bottles shining, surrounded by vines of some sort. I reached in and grabbed a bottle, and one of those vines moved. I fell backward, and it bit me on the leg. It felt like fire, like I'd stuck my calf here directly into a flame."

He rolled up his leg and showed a disproportionately smaller calf with what looked like a furrow of flesh dug out.

"I ran home, and the fire burned and burned harder. I was in the hospital for a week, then I was home, and for the first time in my life, I couldn't go anywhere or do anything. All I could do was lay there and be on fire. I couldn't eat, I could hardly drink, I couldn't talk, I didn't want to move.

"A few days in, once I was no longer in fear of death, there came a long time when all I could do was lie in bed and be in pain. My parents couldn't sit and be with me all day; they had to work, and I knew that that was just life. Now, there was this odd kid who, like me, couldn't stand to be at school. He just went off and hid every day so nobody would bother him and talk to rocks or whatever he did. And one of the things he like to do was play an old out of tune, rusty-string guitar. So seeing as he didn't have any friends, he caught wind that I was stuck in bed, and he would come visit me. I couldn't stand that, but I was too weak and too busy with being on fire to say anything, so he would come in my room and play that rusty, busted up, out of tune guitar.

"After a while I grew a little better and he would let me fiddle with it. He would play a little something and hand it to me, and I would play a little something. We did this for, I couldn't tell you, months. And I'll tell you, there's not another guitar the world has ever seen before or since that had a sound like that, like pure blues. The sound was as weird as he was, jang jang jang. And what else was, he never hardly talked, ever. You could talk to him, but he wouldn't talk back. He was just built that way. That was Rayford. He taught me how to play the blues. The rattlesnake taught me the blues, and Rayford taught me how to *play* the blues. And if that rattlesnake hadn't weakened my leg like that, I wouldn't never have sat still long enough to learn how to play guitar. It's all thanks to that rattlesnake that I became a blues musician instead of winding up in the pen like I was finna do. The day I got bit, my life was changed forever."

"So, *the* Rayford, he was that kid?"

"Yep, same guy, he played on my first tour. Potato and the Spudtones." Potato laugh-coughed. "He would stand there on stage like this, head down, just playing. He truly lived in a dimension of pure blues. He was the best wingman ever, too. All the girls went after him and he didn't give one sweet damn, so me and the boys got the pickings. Then he got into the heroin and I guess that was the first time he ever truly felt good in his life, because he went downhill pretty fast after that. 'I Found Some Fleas' was the last song we wrote together. You getting all this?"

Dominic nodded and took the opportunity to pop in a new microcassette.

"Know what? You need a name. Tapes. That's it. Henceforth and heretofore into the thereafter, I dub thee Tapes Fillmore. Now Tapes, bring me that guitar off the wall up there. The light blue one."

"Isn't this—"

"'Stellaaaaahh!' Because it's a Stella. From 1938. The year Robert Johnson died. That was Rayford's guitar, the very one. Now, it's been fixed up over the years. Don't look under the top, it been fixed all up and back again, it looks worse 'n that old Rock Lick Bridge down the road. Then I added the paint job in Rayford's honor. Pretty soon imma find him up there ignoring all the angels and banging out the hardest licks in all heaven. Tapes, I'm giving this to you."

"Wait, I can't, what about your children and grandchildren?"

"None of 'em play. They'll get the house. They can put up a historical marker and sell tickets. 'This pile of sticks is the used-to-be-home of blues great Potato Jones, as raggedy as he.'" Potato doubled over in a laughing and wheezing fit. The sound of the wheezing just made him laugh harder, until he sounded like a teakettle, tears squeezing from his eyes.

"Now this interview is over because I'm tired. You don't have to go, but I sure am. Give me your arm."

Dominic held out his arm, but Potato's bad leg shook so violently that Dominic had to wrap his arm around old man's chest to move him across the small room and maneuver him onto the bed.

"I'm too old to watch TV, but my dreams are better," he said, closing his eyes. "I'm finna be trading licks with all the greats tonight. China and India and everywhere. I'll turn into a bear or one a them giant lizards, long lizard fingers playing for the pretty lizard ladies on Borneo." His hand fluttered. His voice was getting softer and slower and his words more blurry, a ritardando as he faded into sleep. "That's the kind of dreams I have. Promise me you'll play that guitar. Imma check up on you."

"Yes, yes, of course."

"I don't care where you go, but I won't be here."

Potato closed his eyes.

Dominic's were so wide as evening fell that he imagined them as the white ovals of a cartoon animal in the dark. He listened to the old man breathe until he gave one last peculiar snore, and then the room fell silent.

Dominic sat in the silence for a long time. He realized that he had reached adulthood without the foggiest notion of what to actually do in such a situation. He realized that his experience was limited to receiving a phone call from his mother. Was he supposed to call paramedics, who would have to administer an hour of exhausting indignities for no other reason than to avoid a lawsuit, or police, who might just as easily presume that they were appearing on the scene of a homicide?

Potato's flip phone glowed blue on his nightstand. A message from Wendolyn Jones read, "Good night, Daddy."

After another forever of silence, Dominic replied, *"Goodnight, Angel. Rest easy."* Then he picked up the guitar and headed down the barely improved road back towards the weed-strewn town, where, hopefully, a rented room and hot meal were still available.

The Broken Hearts Club of Lieutenant MacLean

By Igor Kholodenko

"But everybody knows
That a broken heart is blind"

"Little black submarine", © The Black Keys

When Ritty and I walked in our apartment, Grumpy was snoring, as usual, on the couch near the door.

"What a good watchman", with irony said Ritty, "he is snoring so serene, that even a child could rob us, and he won't even open one eye."

Grumpy immediately woke up and grumbled that although he was dozing, he will never allow any stranger to enter in our home. For greater persuasiveness, he bared his impressive fangs and began snoring again.

"You can't change him", said Ritty, "our little tiger cub is a big sleepyhead. Anyway, let's drink some teaoos[1]."

I went into the kitchen to put our kettle on, and sweet tooth Ritty, began unloading on the table sweets, cookies and boxes with watercolors from her rather voluminous bag.

While the kettle is boiling, I will make a small digression and tell you a little about the three of us.

My name is Dan. Daniel McLean. To put it simply, Dan Lean. I am a former flag lieutenant of communications of the very Third Galactic Fleet, which ... Well, you have to know everything if you learned history at your school or a college. And if you are from some distant farming world, where are no normal schools, then read about this in the galactic Libnet. Maybe, I'll tell those stories later, but not now. Because I don't want to write a novel. I my opinion, our life is collection of short stories. When one of them end – the other is begun. So, be patient, please. Every story should have its own time.

A little bit about us. We, all three of us: Dan Lean, Ritty Meowsky, and Grumpy (Guido Garrat) Tigrinny - are The Broken Hearts Club, or BrokHeC for short. Ritty calls it The Broken Hearts Club of Lieutenant McLean, because it was I who founded it.

A little explanation for my readers from distant, only human, worlds, before I'll continue: Ritty is FelineHume – humanlike feline, and Grumpy is TigerHume - humanlike tiger. Their races, among others, were genetically engineered approximately two centuries ago in order to adapt human race to life on planets with climates that very different from Earth's.

So, let's start. When the medical board dismissed almost all of our warship crew, three of us decided to stick together until we settled our personal lives. However, Grumpy was only interested in food and sleep, fortunately his (like mine and Ritty's) benefits of a military pension for a veteran of space battles allowed him to do this. But Ritty and I wanted to find a mate. I wanted to find a pretty blonde girl, and Ritty dreamed of a respectable feline, preferably, also a retired officer, even if not from the space fleet.

"What will I talk about with a civilian jacket?" - often purred she at evenings, curled up in a ball on a large armchair by the fireplace. "He won't understand me, and I won't understand him. I can't have kittens from such a person! May the Great Universe spare me from this!"

But no matter how hard we tried - our amorous affairs didn't go well. Only Grumpy was almost snatched away by one person. Young lady of the tiger race tried to charm him once during a park walk (let me clarify that Ritty and I were walking, and Grumpy was sleeping on park grass), but Grumpy only waved off her advances with his paw and continued sleeping. He once had a loved one, but she abandoned him, and since then, whenever possible, he prefers sleep to reality.

We lived peacefully all together: Ritty was busy with her paintings and drawings, I was digging in new quantum-electronic circuits, Grumpy, if he wasn't sleeping, was watching soccer games.

But one day Ritty suddenly disappeared. I began to worry, after all, she is my fighting friend, but two days later I received a message from her consisting of only five words: "Fell in love! Don't wait for me!" I sent her in a reply message "Be happy!", and, leaving Grumpy at the housework, I went to the nearest bar, where I drank to Ritty's happiness and to my luck, splashing a little from the glass in honor of the fickle Fortune. And, you know, I was lucky. Apparently, Fortune liked that thirty-year-old Oiry[2], because two days later, returning from work through the park, I met there a charming blonde girl. Word by word, a several weeks of dating, and three weeks later Lily and I decided to get married. I rented a small but cozy apartment, leaving the old to Grumpy.

I was looking forward for a happy life. But even a month had not passed, when my beloved wife, who had previously cooed sweetly, lost her angelic voice, and instead she began to growl, grumble, and even squeal. To say that I was dumbfounded is to say nothing. It soon became clear that I was such an such, lazy donkey, dumbhead, cretin and so on. She explained me that other husbands carry their wives in their arms all the time and blow away specks of dust from them, and do not allow tender fingers of their wives even to touch household machines. And they also take them, at least three times a year, to the planet resorts of Eris, Mountrain and Flora. And only I want to slip her something for poor like Canary Islands, Tahiti, and Hawaii. Needless to say, I couldn't stand it for long. I filed for divorce and moved back to Grumpy's in our old apartment. Next day after the divorce I liquored up till my eyebrows, and didn't remember how got back home.

Smell of beautiful coffee woke me up.

With difficulty opening my eyes, I saw a female figure against the background of the window and fear struck me like an electric shock. Could it be Lily?

"Who are you?" I asked rubbing my eyes. "And what are you doing here?"

And I heard Ritty's calm and confident voice.

"Remember for the rest of your life, Dan. If somebody at a morning bring you a cup of nice coffee, just drink it and don't ask silly questions. Yesterday you got so drunk that you couldn't walk. The bartender found your communicator in your pocket and called me. And I stuck here all night, because can't rely on Grumpy in such cases."

Then she left.

And we continued to live with Grumpy as usual. But after month and a half, Ritty joined us.

What happened to her there with her chosen one - I don't know. Only once I tried to ask her a question about this, and her sweet and sad little face instantly changed, she bared her teeth, and from her throat I heard that very fighting roar of the felines, which I heard only during battles. We didn't return to this topic again. Never. Sometimes Ritty grumbled that all male felines were stray dogs, this, apparently, was equivalent to the human saying "all men are goats", but the conversation did not go further than that. That's when I declared us a The Broken Hearts Club. As a joke. But, as people say, there is a grain of joke in every joke, and everything else is true.

***

The water boiled, I prepared the teaoos (I like to brew the teaoos myself, it doesn't come out as tasty with kitchen automats), and went into the living room. Ritty and I drank teaoos with cookies and sweets until midnight. Grumpy was still sleeping, but the two of us didn't feel like sleeping. We sat down in armchairs by the fireplace and began chatting about this and that, remembering our space fleet life, and then Ritty said:

"You know, Dan, I'm so sorry that you're not a feline, I couldn't wish for a better husband."

"Yes, Ritty", I answered, "if you were my kind, I couldn't find a better wife. Sometimes it happens, unfortunately, you meet a good, ummm, friend, but both of you belong to different biological species. I never had a better fighting friend and friend than you, but I absolutely can't imagine how I... We...".

Then I stopped talking and blushed, and Ritty laughed loudly.

"Yeah, you can't argue with biology, and I'll never give birth to kittens from you, and I've seen how are you licking your lips when you seeing young blonde ladies. Don't blush! This is normal. I'm also drawn not to you, but to felines like Elveel. Well, you know, the one from the series "Wild Space", although I know that there's nothing there other than appearance. A beautiful but empty shell."

She was silent for a moment, and then added:

"Nevertheless, make me your wife, Dan. And I'm not kidding."

***

The mayor's office did not want to register our marriage.

"Your species are biologically incompatible," the elderly lady official registrar gently but sternly impressed upon us, "You will never have offspring. Yes, I know that in other worlds there are interspecies marriages, but here on

Earth this is not the case. Basically, I can't register you. Moreover, you don't have a witness."

"Who told you that we don't have one?", objected I and looked out the door and called Grumpy.

"Good afternoon", said Grumpy, entering the office, "I'm ready to be a witness for this cute couple. I hope there won't be any problems with me being a witness?"

At the same time, he smiled, affectionately revealing his huge sugar fangs.

As said once one historical figure, a kind word and a toothy smile can achieve more than just a kind word. The official grumbled a little about the depraved morals of today's youth, but she still registered us. We were already at the door when Ritty turned around and said:

"As for debauchery, this is not about us. We're not going to sleep together. If you've seen too much of some kind of dumb nonsense serials, then all the complaints must be sent to their idiot scriptwriters and their stupid directors. And we just have a friendly partnership marriage."

And she slammed the door with all her might, so pendants on the chandelier in the hall began to dance.

I don't know how the official managed to call about our marriage, but when we left the city hall, reporters were already crowding the steps. Since Grumpy was walking next to us, they did not dare to come close, they just filmed us from afar.

They just clicked buttons of their holographic cameras. Suddenly, a girl of about twenty-five to thirty years old, representative of human race, shouted from the crowd of journalists:

"I am a representative of Feline Rights Watch Marjorie Spotush! Madam Ritty, if the person, who right now next to you, forced you to become his wife, don't be afraid, tell it to us now!"

Like in slow motion I saw how the happy expression on Ritty's face change dramatically, heard the still unclear bubbling in her throat, and already imagined the headlines of evening newspapers:

"Combat officer of laser guns deck of the Third Galactic Fleet, first lieutenant of the reserve, Ritty Meowsky tore into small shreds the clothes and face of a representative of the human race, who is working in FRW!"

Of course, not many persons loved these upstarts from various rights watches, because they always sticking their noses where they shouldn't, and always interpreting and distorting facts as they please. But the law is the law, as said the hero of the famous comedian of the past, Fernandel.[3] Of course, Ritty is a very smart feline and she wouldn't use her claws, but her tongue is very sharp and there could be a lot of trouble.

Suddenly, two of Grumpy's powerful paws gently pushed us behind his back.

"Dear young and too smart lady from FRW", roared Grumpy, "you don't have to shout from afar, you're welcome to come straight here and ask your questions to Missis Ritty. But I have to warn you, if she finds your questions and fabrications offensive, then I will personally spank you below your lower back by my paw for insulting my fighting friend. And there will be no consequences for me, except a week in the hospital, because I have a combat wound of my head. And as for you, please note, that outright fabrications against a military officer, you can be thrown out even from your so-called feline rights watch."

Needless to say, the young defender of feline rights instantly got lost in the crowd amid the laughter of those around her.

And we went home.

When Ritty and I approached our house, I noticed an old man on a bench in the park near the house. It was notorious Scandalletoff. Actually, his name was Candellotoff. Rog Candelotoff. He was once a fairly popular journalist, but then he got into some dark story, retired, and now, if the weather was good, he sat on a bench for days, writing something in his electronic notepad. He received the letter "s" at the beginning of his last name because of his very scandalous character.

Noticing me and Ritty, he immediately started typing something in his notebook. And when we passed by, he hissed, barely audible: "Damned perverts."

If I heard this, then undoubtedly Ritty with her cat's hearing heard it, even though she walked five or six steps ahead of me. Ritty stopped. I froze. But then Grumpy's heavy paws fell on our shoulders again.

"Home," he said quietly, "Go home, I'll sort it out myself."

But we didn't go home, and hid behind a large retro-style poster stand.

Grumpy walked up to the bench where was sitting Scandalletoff and sat down next to him.

"You are absolutely right", said sadly Grumpy. "They are perverts by their nature. How can a human marry a cat, even a humanoid one? Tigers and people are another matter. We are better suited to each other".

With these words, Grumpy put his paws around Scandalletoff's shoulders and gently pulled old man towards his chest.

"If you were younger", continued Grumpy, "we could make a wonderful couple. You must have been such a handsome man when you were young!"

Scandalletoff turned pale. Then he turned gray. He tried to escape from Grumpy's embrace, but it was easier to move the iron cast poster stand, behind which we were hiding, than to unclench Grumpy's steel embrace.

Scandalletoff wanted to say something, but only vague bubbling came out of his throat. After about two or three minutes, Grumpy got tired of playing with this mouse, which had turned even grayer during those minutes, and he let him go. With unprecedented agility for his age, Scandalletoff took off and disappeared into the shadows of the park alley.

Without saying a word, we began to laugh together. And then we went home, where we had a small feast in honor of our marriage.

***

Oh, and there was a huge splash! Photos of me and Ritty constantly flashed on the screens, all kind of media screamed about the first interspecies marriage in the history of the Earth, we were bombarded with offers to participate in various talk shows and radio broadcasts. Now me and Ritty went for a park walk only together with

Grumpy, but still, a crowd often gathered at a distance from us.

And if we went on our businesses, to work or shopping alone, difficult trials awaited us. I don't know how it was for Ritty, I only saw from a distance a couple of times how one or another fluffed-up male feline was following after her.

And as for me, young girls declared a real hunt after me. Are you laughing? But it wasn't funny to me at all. Since I prefer to walk, both to work and for shopping, on my way I constantly came across girls who suddenly twisted their ankle, broke the heel of a shoe, or fainted from the heat right into my arms. And how many handkerchiefs and handbags I had to lift! I was lucky that I didn't visiting a pool or didn't go to a beach, otherwise, instead of relaxing and swimming, I would have had to pull out of the water brunettes, blondes and brown-haired women, thin and not so thin ...

But they had no success in their hunts. Both Ritty and I had no intention of cheating on each other with members of our own species. Well, what I mean about cheating, we lived as before, nothing like what is written about in vulgar novels could have happened between us, we simply valued our friendship and trust in each other.

***

But one day, I finally got hooked, and what's strange is that it wasn't a blonde, but a brunette.

It was happened in the end of September. She was sitting on a park bench and reading a book. When I passed by, I glanced first at the cover and then at the face of the beautiful stranger. The girl was reading Dickens. Notes of the Pickwick Club. She didn't even look at me. My heart sank, but I passed by, walked away, but then returned and sat down on the bench next to her.

"It's a good book, isn't it?" asked I.

The girl looked at me so sternly that I felt how my ears turn red, and I wanted immediately to get up and leave. I don't even know what held me back, but I continued, looking into her sea-blue eyes:

"I re-read this book six times. And among the authors of past centuries, I love Kipling, Chekhov, Gashek, Gogol, Dickens, O. Henry, Simak, Remarque, brothers Strugatsky, Asimov..."

And then the girl looked up from the book and looked at me with great interest in her beautiful eyes. For a moment that she looked at me, I felt that I starting to blush. And then she again staired into her book.

Dusk was slowly falling on the park. Smell of evening dew was in the air. On the dark-blue sky appeared horns of the young, not fully visible yet, Moon. Distant Jupiter began to flicker as dim dot. Soon this girl will close the book, will get up, and will leave. And I, maybe never, will not be able to find her among many million population of our city.

I have no other choice and used my last weapon. I recited my old poem, just changing a few words in it:

The light felicity - the indigo night,

The turquoise melancholy - Her azure eyes,

Cornflower leaves, ultramarine streams,

The far deep blue forest near blue hills,

Violet clouds with a gone thunderstorm,

Twinkle bluish stars and the Moon like a coin,

Is she reality or a wonder for a while?

It's quiet.

There is not a sound, under the fathomless sky."

She raised her head again, in her eyes there were shining lights from recently lit up lanterns.

"Is this your verse?" Asked she almost in a whisper.

I just nodded.

And then we wandered by yellowish-red park alleys until complete darkness, and I recited her my poems from my memory. Like this one, which I made up on the fly:

The Autumn has kitten's paws,

By rustling in fallen leaves,

She follows you everywhere,

With sadness your heart overfills.

She wouldn't allow you smiling,

She never allows you run,

And even near a hot stove,

She never will let you go.

She'll pour near your window,

Herbarium of torn leaves,

And will write a fairy tale story,

With a rain's softly clicks.

She will write on roofs that are yellow,

Then by wind will play a song,

About a summer with a stellar dawn,

And the Moon that like a sugar horn.

She will tell you a long story,

About a dawn that you couldn't see,

Which melted like a chocolate candy,

In a cup of a lemon tea ...

***

Victoria and I, (that was the name of the beautiful stranger girl from the park), got married three and a half months later. A month before, Ritty and I divorced by mutual consent. Ritty was all for it, especially since by that time she often returned home after midnight, sparkling with happy eyes.

Now I can reveal my and Ritty's little secret. That evening, when she asked me to become her husband, and saw my raised eyebrows, she added:

"Don't look at me like that, Dan. I love you as a friend, and like you, I am very tired of being alone. You know what I mean. If we get married, there will certainly be dozens, if not hundreds, of yours and my species who will want to take away one of us. And then be attentive and don't miss a smile of your fortune."

"Stop, Ritty," said I, "I do not think that it going to work. Is it again one of yours new age art performances?"

"Listen, Den, you my best friend, but ..."

"My dear Ritty", interrupted I, "of course, I love you like a friend, but I do not believe this particular idea will give any good results, regardless of any of your art and life goals. Art is not the golden key that unlocks the chest of desires."

"This is about other kind of art, Dan, About art of friendship and empathy. There is no art that can make from a man, or a woman, a Human with big letter "H". You remember that maniac Hitler from 20th century? He was not a bad artist, but he was awful human being. Germany and Russia had a great cultural background. But did that cultural backgrounds really save them from turning into fascist states, when a large part of their population imagined themselves to be a superior race that has the right to kill others just because they do not want to obey them? Did Durer, Goethe, Schiller, Heine, Bach, Beethoven, Kirchner and others help the majority of Germans maintain their humanity and empathy to other nations during the Nazi era? Did Pushkin, Dostoevsky, Tolstoy, Repin, Savrasov, Perov, Aivazovsky, Kandinsky, Tchaikovsky, Shostakovich, Rachmaninov help most of the population of Russia don't turn into scoundrels and supporters of killers of woman and children? Did the entire Earth culture of past centuries help the colonists of Antares not to kill the native population? Neither art of painting, nor art of music or poetry make us humans, but art of friendship and empathy. Humanity began when people learned how to care about each other, about old, sick and wounded, but not when first cave paintings appear. Famous anthropologist of 20th century Margaret Mead once said that human thigh bone with a healed fracture, that was 15,000 years old, was more real sign of civilization than all kind of art of that period. Civilization began when people start to care about each other."

"But how friendship and empathy can be an art? They are just human qualities. Your paintings are an art, but ..."

"Yes, these *qualities* can be art and they will. That is what I want to prove, Dan. And besides this, I promise, you will find your love. Are you with me, my friend?"

***

She saw it in a magic crystal ball. I don't know about Ritty, I'd personally thought that I was lucky not to become the object of a hunt, and to find the loved one myself. And only recently, when we were expecting our first child, Vicky confessed to me.

"Dan, don't be angry... That time in the park I was also hunting for you. Not just like others did. I studied your biography, and even found in your abandoned online diary with a list of books you loved to read. I didn't think I could do it, but ... Are you mad at me, Dan?"

In response, I just hugged her and kissed tenderly her nose.

***

That is how our Club of Broken Hearts ceased to exist. Grumpy was eventually picked up by the very tiger girl who was trying to charm him. She simply impudently kidnapped him from the park - called for transportation and took him to her place. Grumpy didn't even move his whiskers. Ritty's family, mine, and Grumpy's family maintain friendly ties. Grumpy no longer sleeps all day long; he became a famous soccer journalist, and even received the Prize from journal *Soccer*. Ritty now is very important person, but not because of our past marriage, but because now she is founder of empathy art school and her initiative has spread across all inhabited worlds like wildfire. And only I continue to develop quantum-electronic circuits, as before, but what is most important for me and takes most of my time – it is caring about my wife and daughter. And only if I have free time, I'm writing my memoirs.

By the way, I and Ritty are not afraid about our marital status. We now know well about art of empathy, and if anything happens, we always have a welcome ally in each other person. As one poet of past centuries wrote:

"After all, nowhere does it say
What to reliable, great friends
Is it forbidden to get married." [4]

THE END

1 Teaoos – a new type of tea in the future

2 Oiry - a brandy like beverage in the future

3 *The Law Is the Law*—a 1958 French-Italian comedy film directed by Christian-Jaque starring Fernandel and Toto

4 Final lines of the poem "We decided with you to be friends" by a Soviet romantic poet Eduard Asadov

Los Angeles

By Sarah Magnuson

In Chelsea, I'm sitting on a rock outside of Grey Dog, waiting for my son's cheese fries. I'm enjoying a moment alone in the sun, when a long-haired man appears out of the landscaping and walks towards me. I'm not in the mood to speak to a stranger.

"Hey! I don't mean to bother you, but I wanted to tell you that you have an amazing smile! It's lighting up the afternoon. Hey! I like your hair."

At first I think he's just trying to talk to me, but when he says, "I like your hair," I begin to wonder if he is one of the *angels*. That's the phrase they always say to me, and it always sends a chill down my spine.

"Oh, thank you. Yes, I changed it recently."

He says, "So, what are you doing here, on this rock?"

"Just waiting for some cheese fries."

"Oh! Isn't that wonderful? It's a wonderful day, isn't it?"

"Yes, we don't get too many perfect Spring days like this one, do we? Before you know it, the hot and humid weather will be here."

"Yes! Exactly." He nods, looking into the sky. "Right now, everything is perfect, but a time may come when you will be persecuted. You may have trouble with your family, a problem with your son, and with your boyfriend. Just know you are in good company when you are persecuted. I want you to always remember this moment, sitting here, on this rock. No matter how others treat you in the future, stay exactly as you are now, relaxed."

Trouble with my family? A problem with my son? And what does he mean, boyfriend? "Yes, okay! Have a good day!"

The man walks away, and down into the ground.

*

When I'm at the Rite Aid on Pico later that night, a homeless man stands at the bottom of the steps with his hands out. I don't have any cash on me, so I just nod. I get in my car and see him stand there in the dark, perfectly still, with his hands out. Several groups of people walk past

him without acknowledging him. It's cold outside, and dark out there. No one even sees him. All I have on me is $2 in quarters in the car. I hesitate to give him the money. I just don't feel like approaching him with the change.

When I look over again, his form shapeshifts into a more lively homeless man with a boombox playing loud music. This man is not still and quiet. He moves all over the place, and is he speaking profanities? He dances, and he plays with an invisible basketball. A couple gives him some money on their way out of the store. Another couple walks right through him, as if he isn't even there.

I had more sympathy for the still and silent figure, but this is the same person, just with a different appearance. I don't know why it's so hard to bring myself to give him the quarters. It feels embarrassing, but finally I think, just do it already! I drive over to him in my Jeep and roll down the window.

He sees me and slowly rises from the steps, until he stands over seven feet tall. His attire is elegant, and his countenance, regal. With a graceful, deliberate walk he approaches my open window. His form is not quite human, and his movement occasionally breaks into a collection of still images as in an old black and white movie, as if it takes effort to move through time. His skin is dark, and brilliant light glows around him.

I look into his face, and his face has an indescribable supernatural beauty that is almost painful to look upon. He holds out his hands, and I drop the quarters into it.

They pass through his hands and disappear into the air. A thundering voice beyond everyday worldly experience says, "Thank you, my dear! This will help a lot."

I'm terrified and frozen, unable to speak. So many thoughts swim through my mind. I recall the warning from the angel in at the hot dog stand in Chelsea. "A time may come when you will be persecuted." It was a premonition before the problems started. Now what is the meaning of this new and powerful angel? In my mind, the sky opens up to pink clouds, as in a sunrise.

*

At home, I find two $1 bills in my purse. This is so freaky! What am I supposed to do with this money now? I give the $2 to my daughter. "Here. Take it. An angel gave it to me."

Mia takes the money. "Okay, thanks!"

I feel gratitude for the angel's protection, but also a sense of impending doom. I think about my son, who biked to a friend's house.

*

On Sunday afternoon, outside of Rite Aid, a man is standing by the fence in the parking lot. As I approach the entrance to the store, he transports from the parking lot to standing right beside me. He has a round face, and he wears a nice tan sweatshirt. It's another angel.

He says, "Will you take me to Yoshinoya?"

"Sorry, I'm in a rush today. Can I get you something from inside the store?"

"You'll buy me food from Rite Aid, but not from Yoshinoya?"

"Yeah. Do you want something from Rite Aid?"

"Actually, yes. Can you get me a large pack of anti fungal foot cream? The one in the black package, the largest one they have?"

"Okay. Sure."

On the way out of the store, I hand the angel the foot cream, and he is delighted. "You remembered! And you got the large pack! It's rough out here, you know. Thank you!"

"Okay. You're welcome."

*

Next Sunday afternoon, the angel lurks in the alleyway behind Yoshinoya. He is wearing a new black and tan jacket. He waves brightly. "I remember you! You got me the foot cream. Hey, can you give me some money for Yoshinoya? I'm hungry."

"Sorry, I don't have much cash on me today. I only have a couple dollars."

"Okay. But I remember that foot cream!" He's polishing off a meal from Yoshinoya, eating out of the plastic containers.

*

From then on, every time I stop by Rite Aid, the angel is there, and he always speaks to me. I give him a dollar or two. He is young, well fed, and his clothes are always new. Is he homeless? He never appears to be, but he is always there asking for food.

One day, he's laughing and smiling with a couple on their way into Yoshinoya. Good. Someone else is buying his lunch. It's not all up to me. Maybe I can avoid him today, but he stops and turns his head towards me. "Foot cream!! I remember you! Hi!"

"Hi."

I just want to be able to get everything we need from Rite Aid without having to see this angel every time. Is he an angel? I know for certain the other vision was an angel, a beautiful archangel with a glorious face and supernatural voice that thundered from the sky. I saw him shapeshift right in front of me, and I felt his power deep in my bones. He was truly a supreme being, and I know he's protecting me. Who is this new entity? Is he a human? Why does he recognize me? It creeps me out.

I pray, "Please God. I don't want to see this angel every time I leave the store."

Thank God, he's not there when I exit the store. I gather my wits about me, and I stop by Taco Bell. A long-haired homeless man is there by the exit. His face is bright, and his eyes are shining blue. Oh God, here we go again. He waits right by my car window. I have an extra burrito that I don't really need. I give it to him, to his beaming face. I've had it though. I just want a normal life.

"Hey, I like your hair! That's a new style for you, isn't it? God bless you." And he passes right through the car.

*

It's around 10 pm, inside my condo in Santa Monica. I tell Mia, "Hold on! Let me see if I can find it down here."

On my way down the stairs, I stop suddenly. A man's face is pressed against the glass patio door. He sees me on the stairs, and we lock eyes. He has a round face, and he wears a black sweatshirt and a tan beanie. We are both frozen, waiting to see who's going to make the first move. I hold my ground. I don't want to show any fear. He's staring at me, caught, also unsure of what to do.

"Hey, Mia! There's someone here in the backyard. I might need you to call the police, okay?"

"What? Did you find it yet, Mom?"

"No. I can't find it right now. There's a man in the backyard."

"What? What man? Where is he?"

"He's right here. Can you get your phone? Get ready to call the police."

"What? Can't you call from your phone? I'm kinda texting someone right now." It's almost like Mia thinks I'm playing a game.

"No. I don't want to turn my back on him. I don't know what he might do."

The man turns away and exits my yard. I race up the stairs, so I can keep an eye on him from the vantage point of the glass wall in the living room. I see him standing inconspicuously, turned sideways, hiding, with his back against the neighbor's wall. He waits there quietly, like a cat.

Mia comes running down from her loft. "Where's the man?"

"He's right there. See him hiding by the wall?"

"Oh, I wanna see! Where is he? Where? Where?"

"Right there."

"That person? Oh, I see him! Oh! Look at him! That guy by the wall, right? What happened? He was in the backyard?"

"No, he was down in the patio looking right into the house."

The man walks down the sidewalk and into the night.

*

On Tuesday afternoon, across from John Adams Middle School in Santa Monica, we stop by Bob's Market after school. Then, we pick up my son's bike from the repair shop and ride home through mist and salty air. Why am I tortured by bittersweet memories? Life's far from normal, but I had them with me, my babies. They were right there, both of them, and we had joy and laughter. What's more? What more do you want out of life?

In the evening a few days later, the angel is right beside me by the entrance of the 99-Cent store. I feel trapped. What is he doing here? He asks for money. I decline. I try to get away from him and into the store.

"Hey, hey! Wait! I saw you at Bob's Market. Why didn't you talk to me?"

"What?"

"Yeah. Bob's Market, the other day. Weren't you there? I saw you! How is your son doing? Is everything alright with your son?"

I go into the store. Upon leaving, I'm relieved he isn't there. I see him across the street by the bus stop, looking dejected. I take another route home, so my path won't cross his again.

I Am a Rock

By Edna O'Brien

No one is coming to save me, so I might as well make the best of it. I had no business up there or down here, and I came crashing back down anyway. I recall once reading in a book that the flight of man is a mutiny against God, but I do not believe he has had anything to do with all of this.

I have never been particularly interested in time, so I stopped trying to track its passage after I found the pilot. I broke a long, jagged piece from what remained of the plane's body and used it to dig six feet into the thick, wet soil at the mouth of the green. Esteban was a good man; I would have liked to have flown with him again.

My time on this island is much like you would imagine: hunting, sleeping, finding water, keeping warm, and keeping cool. I use my tool for all of it, spearing lesser beings and sparking fire from nothing. I am the one who is God here.

The looming canopy of the dark jungle obstructs my view of the shore and the rest of the island, but I have made myself comfortable in its palm.

The first time I saw her, the contrast of her pale skin against the void knocked the wind out of me, and I fumbled for my tool in the darkness. She was gone just as quickly as she appeared, if she was ever really there at all. I put out the remaining embers of my fire and sat shivering and terrified through the night. She left me once, and now she has left me again.

I decided to make my way to the other side of the island in the coming days. All I need is my tool, and to trust my jungle.

***

Early on, I am confronted by a thicket of green that seems impenetrable, but not for me or my tool. I begin hacking through, fashioning the jagged metal into a crude machete. I find a rhythm and gain momentum, hacking and hacking until a glimpse of white catches my eye through the chaos of the branches. I know it is her and I stop. The branch I was hacking whips back, carving a gash into the flesh directly over my broken heart. I feel stupid, weak, and tired, and then I keep making my way through to find her.

When I break through, I hear a song I have never heard in my dark pocket of the jungle. I see flashes of purple darting from one thick green branch to another, and I understand what they mean when they say, "bird of paradise." For the first time, I am struck by the beauty of where I have landed myself. I want to hear the song, so I follow it, moving forward.

I hear the water first and see it second, a clear, cool stream that must be making its way to the mouth of the ocean. I lay in the water, letting it wash over the dirt, blood, and sweat. The cut on my chest stings and so does the heart underneath it. I turn over onto my belly and take big gulps of the water just like you would imagine a man on a deserted island might, scooping it up stupidly into my mouth with my tool. I see my reflection in the water, the overgrowth of beard and hair, sun-beaten skin, gaunt cheeks, and dead eyes. I do not recognize him and do not want to look at him anymore.

I want to keep moving but settle in for the dark night. I think about my reflection.

I am not a good man. I have become selfish, single-minded, and mean. When she comes back to me tonight, I will ask her if she meant it when she said that. I will wait for her until I fall asleep to tonight's performance of the bugs and birds.

I dream of her walking out of the home we made together into the cool wet jungle, into the greens, yellows, blues, and birdsong that I did not let myself notice until today.

***

I wake up with a fat cylinder of sandpaper on my face. I blink my eyes, dumb, seeing spots in my half-sleep. I cannot blink them away.

The sandpaper is a tongue, the spots are fur, and the teeth are smiling. My mind briefly flashes to the city zoo, the pathetic and apathetic lions and tigers hunkered behind the thick glass. I do not know if I have ever seen a jaguar, but I am seeing one now, and I feel genuine fear for the first time since I fell to earth in fire. For the first time, I want to go home.

My tool is nowhere, so I get up slowly and back away from the cat. She is truly beautiful, one of nature's sleekest models, and she would take my breath away if she had not already. She turns around and slinks away in her way, and when she turns her blazing amber eyes to look at me, I know to follow her along the length of the water where I saw yesterday the man that I have become here in my jungle.

I am trying to keep up with the rhythm of her movement, but this is her domain, and I cannot move as quickly as she does within the confines of my human body.

She is patient, looking back occasionally to ensure I am still catching up. I am scrambling over roots and rocks, exhausted. The trust in my jungle I set out with is wavering; I am being tested and failing.

I try to keep my gaze between the divine machinery of the jaguar's body and the jungle floor. I see Day-Glo fungi spreading over the mossy rot of the fallen trees; I see fat beetles, the color of the sun shining on oil pooled in a parking lot. I hear the screech of monkeys in the canopy above me and I smell the green and the sweetness of the decay at the foot of it all. The jungle is teeming with squirming, imperceptible life from top to bottom and all sides. It dawns on me that the jungle is not mine and never was.

The jaguar and I are losing light and the leaves above me are turning into ink. She moves faster, and I struggle behind her. My foot gets caught in the thick of two roots. By the time I free myself and look up, my friend is gone.

There is another layer to the symphony I hear, and I become frantic when I realize it is the clear white noise of waves cresting and crashing.

I am running now, and every muscle in my body is on fire. I am thrashing through the vines along the water and find that I am crying, tears streaming down my face and neck and onto my chest. I am searching desperately for a flash of white among the trees. When I realize she is not coming to help me and that she was never here to begin with, I run faster because I am free.

I break through the trees and make it to the beach just in time to see the hot pink sun journey down into the horizon, swallowed up by the sea until tomorrow. The sky looks like God opened his personal paint palette for me to peek into, with colors I couldn't have imagined in my wildest dreams. It cracks me open at the ribs, and I let it all flood in.

Electric, screaming pinks bleed into velvety salmon, tinged on the tips with flamingo feathers. Cosmic carnations, a newborn's fingernail, the inside of oyster shells after you have eaten the meat, capital F-fuchsia, and the purple feathers of the jungle's master soloist, all cascading down. The sun sinks faster when you don't want to meet the night. I would choose to never see a crisp blue sky again if it meant taking this in just one more time.

I want to paint it, but it's not on my palette. I do not recall ever wanting to paint before, and I laugh for what feels like the first time since I became this man.

Along the tiny hairline fracture where the sea meets the sky, I can just barely make out pillars of smoke rising up into the dripping paint from the ship that is coming to bring me home. I feel my body pulling backward, back into the gaping mouth of the jungle to the man I have been. It takes the last of what I have to keep moving toward the white lace of the waves creeping up the sand, scream, and wave my arms up and down.

The world is beautiful, and I want to be a good man.

Crown Vic

By Devin Olson

Vernon's shoes would never recover from this level of staining. The growing pool of blood crept its way around his feet, seeping into the fabric of his white New Balance sneakers. Vernon's face, spattered and wet from blood, sank low and grew pale. The blood dripped down his cheeks as it mixed with his tears.

"Not like this. Not like this!" He pleaded to himself.

Looking around for an escape or solution, Vernon couldn't help but lock eyes with the man in the photos around the room. The grinning face of the now dead man smiled at Vernon with a look he had never given him before, and standing beside the man in each photo was Vernon's ex-wife Cassidy. Out in the hall, Vernon could hear clacking footsteps charging up the stairs. "Jeremy?" a young voice called out.

Quickly, with no hesitation, Vernon raised his handgun to his chin. A 5-round snub-nosed revolver. Well, it was 5, now it's 4. Once upon a time, it was standard police issue, just like Vernon's company car, a 2006 Crown

Victoria. A real beauty to the right person. Vernon was that person.

Just twenty minutes earlier, Vernon was nestled within that very car, parked across the street from the house he found himself standing inside. He was only there to keep watch. That's all he ever wanted to do was watch; at least that's what he always told himself. But recently, Vernon had learned something, something he wouldn't be able to forget. It was during those days when Vernon had nothing going on that he liked to park near that house. Just to watch. On this day, he saw something that he knew he shouldn't have. As his ex-wife and her new partner moved into their home, 32660 Bradley Lane if you care to know like Vernon did, they set out a lovely garden gnome with his hands held close to his lips, making that face we all make when we go "shhh." You know the one. As Vernon watched, he saw them place something under the gnome. There could be no mistaking what the item was. Not something big, but something incredibly small. "Shhhh." This, of course, would be his secret.

For days, Vernon's heart raced and pounded in his chest. He was unable to focus at work and could only think of one thing: the item that lay beneath the garden gnome. His cursed thoughts intruded the forefront of his mind like smoke pluming around a door, seeping into every crack and poisoning it with thoughts of only one thing. One dark and damnable thing.

Vernon couldn't recall when it happened or even how, but he found himself parked outside of their house once again. Not much going on this morning, no activity around the house. Vernon checked his Facebook on his phone, but of course, he knew better than to just check on his own. Since the trial, his ex-wife had blocked him. But, lucky for Old Vernon, she never blocked his sister: Veronica.Gareth@hotmail.com. EBHS2003! Vernon's muscle memory allowed him to enter his sister's login information very quickly, but he did this much more than he should have. Just as quickly, he scrolled through to his ex-wife's page. Cassidy Jones. Vernon thought Cassidy Gareth sounded much better than Cassidy Jones. She had changed her name as soon as she married this guy, and her profile photo had been their wedding portrait ever since. Seeing that picture grew a pit in Vernon's stomach. Jeremy Jones, ugh. To see Jeremy with his wife, I mean ex-wife, stung just as much today as it did twelve months ago.

But hang on—what's this? A new post from Cassidy: "Off to Cancun for my first conference!" Cassidy wasn't home.

Bleep! Bleep! The white suburban parked in the driveway of 32660 Bradley Lane flashed as the trunk opened slowly on its own. Flying out of the house, a small boy in a soccer jersey and cleats shouldered a bag to the trunk before throwing it in the back and running to the front of the car.

"Vernon!" another voice called out from within the house. Vernon slumped down deep into his seat.

"I want to sit in the front!" With that, the young boy moped his way to the back of the car.   Before long, Jeremy came running out the front door. "Come on kids. We gotta go; we're running late now."

Vernon hated the sound of this man's voice. He prided himself in knowing that his voice was deeper than Jeremy's. That kind of thing mattered to Vernon. Seeing this man take care of his children was like a hot knife in Vernon's heart. Everything Vernon once did, now this man did. Making dinner for his family, playing games with his children, and making love to his wife. This man replaced him in every way.

As Jeremy's white suburban drove away, Vernon leapt from his car and made a line for the house with no doubt in his movement. As he crept up to the house, Vernon sputtered hateful nonsense at Jeremy, spiteful for the life he now lived. Before he reached the house, he stopped to delicately lift back the garden gnome to reveal his secret. A small golden key. The key to the house. Like a feral cat, Vernon leapt to the front porch and slid the key into the lock. It was a perfect fit. The door unlocked with a hollow click and then opened without a sound. Once inside, he locked the door behind him.

Everything about this space seemed familiar to Vernon. He remembered being dragged along to the store to find a set of drapes that matched the furniture his wife had picked out. That's the couch where he would pass out after getting home from work. He could sleep there for hours, and not a thing could wake him. But on the walls and the end tables, all these photos were so strange to him. Everywhere he looked he saw Jeremy with Vernon's family. The CD rack that Vernon spent days going from Best Buy to Best Buy looking for was now filled to the top with Jeremy's CDs. Vernon never could quite fill it up. As he made his way to the kitchen, Vernon saw a wall of awards, certificates, and accolades, all with the same name. Jeremy Jones. What a prick, Vernon thought, showing off to his kids.

It was then Vernon saw her. The woman across the street. Her white hair frizzed around her face. She seemed to be looking right at him, her milky eyes staring deep into Vernon's soul. Could she see him? The real him? He felt magnetized, pulled to the place he stood by a force not his own. But time passed and the woman did nothing. Maybe she couldn't see him; maybe she couldn't see at all. All Vernon knew was that whatever kept him from moving seemed to have passed, and in a flash, he launched himself up the stairs and passed another wall of photos. He saw his children's rooms, like a copy and paste from their old home. His daughter's room seemed pinker than he remembered, but he never really noticed before now. Across the hall, with the door ajar and a robe hanging over it, was the master bedroom. Vernon's heart pounded in his chest like never before. His palms sweat profusely; he could barely grip the door.

Although she was out of town, Vernon could still smell his ex-wife's perfume in the air. The sheets and comforter weren't the same, but the smell of her was still there. It had been months since Vernon last remembered smelling her. When the judge upheld the restraining order, it was kind of the last straw. Now he couldn't even see his own kids. Vernon caught a glimpse of something he recognized, a bookmark on the left nightstand, the one Cassidy always used to keep her place in her books. Vernon grabbed the pillow by her side of the bed and clenched it close to his face, breathing in deeper, filling his lungs until they felt as if they would burst, leaving him lifeless with his final thoughts being of her. If only.

Vernon lay back on the bed as he rolled around thinking about his wife. Their old life together. The moments they shared alone. The time before they had children. He stopped abruptly in his intense writhing and reached for the nightstand drawer. His hand drew out a small silk pouch. Of course. She still kept her toys in the same place. He clicked a button, and the bag buzzed. Vernon smiled ear to ear as tears filled his eyes. Suddenly, from outside, Vernon heard the screeching of tires and the hum of a large car as it came to a halt.

Pulling into the driveway was the white suburban. Muffled from outside, Vernon heard a man's voice. "I am so sorry—I know exactly where it is upstairs. Just sit tight." Jeremy launched himself out of the car and into the house. Vernon froze once again, eyes darting side to side as if to find some sort of salvation around him. On the dresser by the window, Vernon locked eyes onto a thick leather wallet. As he opened it up, looking right at him was the government-issued identification card belonging to one Mr. Jeremy Jones. Organ Donor. The bedroom door swung open as if hit with a gust of wind, and as he was running through the doorway, Jeremy stopped dead in his tracks. 'Vern? What the hell are you doing here?"

Without thinking, Vernon reached his hand into his jacket pocket and pulled out his small snub-nosed revolver. Just as quickly as it was drawn, Vernon fired the gun. It only took a few seconds before blood began to spill out from beneath Jeremy's fingers and hands. Although he gripped his neck as tightly as he could, it didn't make a difference. The bullet hit his jugular. What more could anyone do? As Jeremy fell to his knees, the reality of what happened began to set in. What did I just do? Vernon only bought that gun so he could feel more like a cop. With the car, and the gun, and maybe if he got a jacket, then he really would seem tough–at least that's what Vernon thought. This wasn't supposed to happen.

"What have I done? What have I done?" Vernon repeated to himself over and over as he paced back and forth, when suddenly, Vernon slipped his foot into the growing pool of blood. He stopped in place as to not track it around, but quickly it began to surround his shoes. They were his nice shoes too, the ones he wore on his days off. Looking down at Jeremy, Vernon thought, How could one guy bleed so much? I doubt I'd bleed that much.

From outside, Vernon heard a car door slam shut as clacking footsteps made their way inside and up the stairs. With no choice left, Vernon took his revolver and placed it against his chin. "Not like this!" As the clacking shoes made their way closer and closer, Vernon closed his eyes as he took in one final breath before pulling the trigger. But something was wrong, very very wrong. He pulled the trigger and there was nothing. Not a fucking thing. Nothing but a click. He pulled the trigger back again and again. Nothing. Flustered, Vernon began to cry, but not just tears down his cheeks, a full blown meltdown and panic. "Fuck, fuck, fuck. What the hell? No, no. Wait. No, no, no..." Vernon tried again and again, but still nothing.

"Jeremy?" The clacking shoes took their final steps through the doorway, into the room. "Dad? What are you doing here? What's Jeremy doing?" The boy saw the gun in Vernon's hand and then the growing pool of blood coming from Jeremy's motionless body.

"I can explain, I can explain!" Vernon pleaded.

His son, choking back tears: "What did you do, Dad?" The boy stepped back, dragging his soccer cleats through the blood before running out of the room and down the stairs.

"Wait, wait. Please, wait! Just wait, son. Please!"

Vernon tripped and squirmed on the ground, pulling himself up through the blood and grabbing the keys to Jeremy's suburban. "Just stop, son, please!"

As Vernon came crashing out the front door, he expected to leave the Crown Vic behind, get into Jeremy's car, and drive off into the sunset with his kids. If his ex-wife wanted to start a new life without Vernon, then Vernon was going to start a new life without her, and the kids would be his. He would get a home, get the kids in a good school, and live like they used to. Stumbling down the entryway stairs, Vernon was met with the butt end of a shotgun—police issue—as three officers swarmed the area and got on top of him, digging their knees deep into his back.

"Clear him of his weapon, cuff him up tight, and then get his ass into the back of the squad car."

The blood that covered Vernon's body left behind trails everywhere he went. As the police drove him away, Vernon scanned the area. Across the street, the old woman with milky eyes stood talking with a police officer. She pointed straight at Vernon, nodding her head. His children looked upon him with fear on their faces and tears in their eyes. The squad car protected Vernon from hearing the true horror of their wailing.

The Final Application

By Tvisi Ravi

The screen dims and brightens with the same piercing light each time he hits the refresh button. And still, the word glaring back at him in capital letters is not "accepted." It is not "rejected," "waitlisted," or "deferred;" simply "pending."

It is written in a font that exudes prestige, with letters standing tall and intimidating on the page. Each curve arcs with deliberate purpose, making the word uncharacteristically decisive. Pranav Mohaan has encountered this word sixteen times, on sixteen different pages, always while sitting in the same spot at his desk, wearing the same pair of lucky boxers. He is all too familiar with what follows on the screen.

Dear Pranav, The Office of Admissions has completed our review of your application, and I am very sorry to inform you that we cannot offer you admission to the Class of 2028. I wish a different decision had been possible, but receiving a final decision now will be helpful to you as you make your college plans. While the Office conducted its deliberations with the utmost care, we know that no one can predict with certainty what an individual will accomplish during college or beyond. Experience suggests that what students do over the next four years to develop their personal strengths and talent is far more important than the particular colleges they attend.

At this rate, he would be satisfied with *any* college, let alone a *particular* one. This had only sometimes been the case. Until a few months ago, he had been determined to attend Stanford University, far from his small town in New Jersey. He dreamt of playing club tennis in warm weather year-round, sitting on the grass next to a pile of bicycles and books, with a large group of friends—future diplomats and Olympic medal winners. He imagined joining a dance team, something he'd been too afraid to do in high school. He applied to Stanford early but received a resounding rejection. Quickly, yet painfully, he moved on to other options, submitting a total of seventeen applications. One by one, the rejection notifications arrived, leaving Pranav with a dreadful feeling that he would not receive a single college acceptance. What would he do then? The screen he sits staring at now would determine his fate: the final application.

Pranav watches a spider make its way across his keyboard and over his fingertips. He does not care to move. The thread-like creature crawls from his laptop to the edge of the window in front of him, vanishing behind a plant. Pranav's gaze shifts to the street outside, where his father is clipping the hedges, something he does ritualistically every Saturday, no matter the weather. Today, the sun shines warmly, and the susurrus of the oak tree suggests a pleasant breeze. Yet nothing about this day feels pleasant to Pranav. He wishes for storm clouds and torrential rains. His father reaches for a towel in his back pocket, dabs at the sweat on his face, and looks up at the house. Noticing his son, he calls for Pranav to come down and lend a hand.

"Not now, Dad! School stuff!" Pranav shouts back, pointing at his laptop. His father shakes his head and continues sifting through branches.

Pranav had dreaded telling his father about his Stanford rejection. He delayed it for as long as he could, bracing for the inevitable disappointment. But when the moment came, his father's response was startlingly gentle—a hearty pat on the back and a few reassuring words. His father, famous for his long-winded speeches, had once spent an entire evening lecturing him on the virtues of an engineering degree. Engineering provided stability, he told Pranav. Ironically, his software engineer father had been laid off a decade into his career and struggled to find consistent work after that. Pranav's mother provides for the family.

It was she who encouraged Pranav to apply to Stanford, even though it meant he would be thousands of miles away from her. His mother had moved to the United States to study medicine in San Francisco. Her stories of young adulthood in the Bay Area made Pranav dream of escaping the cold East Coast winters. During college application season, she stayed up late with him, brainstorming essay topics and editing paragraphs. They spent more hours together in those few weeks before the final application deadline than at any other time in Pranav's high school years.

These days, Pranav does his best to avoid both of his parents. Each night, he listens to his mom's footsteps pacing the hallway outside his room. He waits for her to rush in without knocking, as she often does, but instead, she retreats to the kitchen. Later, he would hear a soft knock on the door. He'd open it to find a tray of murukkus and a cup of steaming tea, the mixture of cardamom and ginger immediately filling the room. He always made sure to finish everything on the tray despite having lost his appetite months ago.

Another spider crawls across the desk. Or is it the same one as before? They look nearly identical, though this one appears slightly more prominent, with a peculiar vomit-colored tint. Its ghoulish look compels Pranav to spring back from his chair. He snatches a slip of paper from the floor and swings it at his desk. In one swift blow, he demolishes the creature. He glances at his weapon, expecting to see a spray of green juice left behind, but the paper, a postcard from his cousin Hanaa, is still as clean as before. Strange.

The front of the postcard showcases an image of a grand white building with intricate etchings on its façade. In messy cursive handwriting, there is a long letter from Hanaa on the back. She had fallen in love with the Middle East. Her body had quickly acclimated to the weather, and she had become friendly with a local family who took her to the best places to eat. She confessed that she wanted to stay longer and get involved with a local non-profit but worried about what her parents would think.

Pranav has always admired Hanaa for leaving college and pursuing her dream of traveling around the world. He once visited her at Yale in her second semester freshman year. This was just a few months before she officially dropped out, but even then, Pranav sensed something wasn't right. He thinks back to a quiet moment in the dorm room with her after returning from a party, both still a bit hazy from the alcohol. They were making their way through a box of nachos they picked up from Taco Bell.

"So what did you think of the party?" she asked him, breaking the silence.

"It was fun. I liked meeting your friends," he said.

"Friends. Ha," she said, scoffing. "I'm not sure I would call them my friends."

"What do you mean?" Pranav looked at her with a raised eyebrow. Earlier in the dining hall, she introduced him to six or seven different people, girls and boys from her hall or her classes, who showed up excited to meet one of Hanaa's family members. The group squeezed in at a table, and Pranav listened to them share stories. From what he gathered, Hanaa was the most outgoing girl in the hall. She was the one who hosted the pregame before a night out, making sure everyone was included in the festivities. When they sang Backstreet Boys at 2 AM on the way back from a party, she was always the loudest voice in the group. It was Hanaa who made sure her two roommates went to bed with a glass of water on their nightstands, waking them up the next morning for breakfast and a long study session. Pranav was proud of his cousin. He was proud to see that she had friends who appreciated her kindness and saw all the wonderful things about her, things he had loved since they were young children.

When he turned to her, he saw that Hanaa had started crying—softly, without making a noise or displaying any real change in her expression.

"Hanaa?" Pranav moved closer to his cousin, placing a hand on her shoulder. Hanaa wiped away the tears.

"I'm alright. Really, don't worry about it," she said, sitting up taller. "You know there was a girl a few buildings down from here that tried to kill herself recently? She was a freshman, just like me. I think I saw her in my Psych class. I don't know what happened to her, but I think she survived. Thank God. Anyway, don't fall for it, Pranav. College is great, but sometimes, I don't know, it all seems like a big hoax."

He wondered what she meant by that but decided not to probe further.

A month after his visit, Hanaa dropped out. This was back when he was a junior in high school. He remembers being stuck in a never-ending cycle of exams—AP tests, SATs, finals, and so on. At the time, his mind often drifted back to the conversation with Hanaa in her dorm room. He contemplated what it would be like to not go to college. To follow Hanaa's footsteps, probably see the world a bit. He wouldn't have to suffer through any more tests, applications, boring classes, or grueling assignments. He could be free.

But not go to college? The thought now seems otherworldly to Pranav. After all the years he has spent preparing for this moment, he cannot stop. All the Saturdays he could have been with friends instead spent at home with his textbooks. All the afternoon tennis practices, trekking up and down the coast to play in various tournaments, leading his team to state championships this year, all the while maintaining his grades and keeping up with chores and volunteering at the local YMCA for extra credit and...! Well, no, there's no turning back now.

And yet, here he is, with just a single application left. He thinks it does not seem fair, but there is nothing he can do except wait for these ominous letters to turn from 'pending' into something else.

He sits back at his desk, looking out the window at his father, slinging fallen branches into a black plastic bag. The clouds begin to gray as Pranav watches time move by slowly in his cul-de-sac. Neighbors who had been out on their evening stroll make their way back inside. A stray dog trots by and lifts its leg up against the trash bag Pranav's father had set out in front of the house.

As he watches the scene outside, Pranav begins to drift in and out, only barely able to keep himself awake. A sharp chill moves up his spine. His screen has been dark now for hours, but an image is coming to life behind the blackness. He sees the cracked edges of a fingernail first, and then another, and then a rusty and green hand moves slowly through the screen and straight to his throat. He stares in awe, unable to lift his own hands, now tightly squeezing the edges of his desk. The hand wraps itself around his neck, gripping him harder and harder until he can barely breathe. In a matter of seconds, the hand grows to cover his whole body, lifting him up from his chair and holding him suspended in mid-air.

This is it. This is the sweet relief he needs. The sign that it is not meant to be. He would not have to suffer embarrassment once he inevitably finds out he has been rejected once again, that he has no more options, nowhere else to turn to, and no more life ahead of him. He closes his eyes and feels the temperature of his body rise. For the first time in months, he begins to relax.

And then he is on the ground. Released from the hand's grip, he lands on the carpet with a thud. He feels the back of his head. A throbbing pain oscillates so loudly in his skull that he does not hear the rush of footsteps outside.

His mother enters the room. She stands towering over him, brows deeply furrowed, holding a tray of food. She bends down by his side.

"Pranav, are you alright? What happened? What was that noise? Did you fall?" She spouts one question after another, not waiting for a response.

He looks up at his mother's face, then up to the ceiling, where he had been floating moments ago. The hand is no longer there, but a fog of dust hovers above him. His computer, left open on his desk, emanates a green tint from behind the black screen.

"I'm alright, Mom; I just fell from my desk, I guess," Pranav interrupts, sitting up.

"Did you faint? You have not been eating enough; you look so skinny; you need to eat more, Pranav," she says. And finally, she pauses. She cups a hand around his cheek and strokes his face slowly with her thumb.

He looks at his mother. He notices that she, too, has grown thin. Somehow, she seems much younger to him, like she probably looked before he was born, back when she was living in San Francisco. For a brief moment, he imagines his mother out on a great expanse of a grassy field, sitting with friends, talking sweetly and laughing with one another against the backdrop of the Golden Gate Bridge. He imagines himself there as well. He lets out a long breath. He can feel the tension around his shoulders start to give way. He realizes what he could do if it did not work out as planned.

A knock on his door, and his father enters.

"Pranav, you received something in the mail," he says.

His father holds out an envelope. Written in bold letters is the name of the college he has been waiting to hear from all day. Pranav squints at the thin blue ink in the corner of the page. He can barely make out the word,

but he is confident it did not read "pending" or "rejected,"
but instead—

     END

Catching Shadows

By Liz Ogaz Ruiz

The saguaros stood like sentinels in the beauty of the Southwestern desert while the wind howled into the emptiness. The tumbleweeds danced.

Luna was at home, getting all dolled up. She never looked her best first thing in the morning. She checked the clock, afraid she would miss what she termed her *date of destiny*.

Time to get going.

The first rays of dawn emerged on the horizon. Luna's heart skipped a beat. It had been a year since they last met. *Would he look the same? Did he change his hairstyle? Get a trim?*

Their last encounter didn't go so well. Someone came between them. But times change, and this time, *there would be no one to get in their way*. Or so she thought. This time they were the only ones who could blow it.

Of course, there used to be a time when human sacrifices occurred during their *dates*. But now, those stone sites were in ruins, making it hard to imagine that it ever happened, except for the petroglyphs that persisted as reminders. One such Native American rock art was *Piedra del Sol* (Rock of the Sun), a large boulder depicting a circle with looping lines, similar to a sun's corona and thought to represent the total eclipse of July 11, 1097. Nowadays, the children of Earth seemed less interested in looking up and more concerned with looking down at the small boxes they held in their hands. They seemed to be more interested in destinations than journeys.

In the blazing sun, Luna's lips felt parched. Not a good look for her lipstick. Then a voice came from below. It was not from her boyfriend, but from Luna's rival, Terra, who shook and grumbled.

"Foolish Luna. Trying to block my view."

"Hush! Go away, Terra. This is our date of destiny."

You are too small for him. I live in the day. You. A night owl."

"Alas, but here I am."

"Don't be so bold, so arrogant, to think you can play such an important role. You are nothing but a cold and barren satellite. Unlike me, you hold no life."

But as Luna got closer and closer to Corona, her meteor-shaped eyes lit up as her shadow began swallowing him.

Luna was surprised at the quickness of her growing success. Then she blushed, recalling Terra's words. *Who was she, so small, to pull attention away from her beloved?* To hide her face, she draped herself in passing clouds.

Terra said, "Now you've done it, Luna. What does your beloved think of you now? Has he bitten his tongue?"

"He's not a talker, but a man of action."

But deep down in Luna's heart, she wondered if Corona was bothered by her actions.

Just then, as the shadow began swallowing Corona from Terra's view, Corona swathed Luna with beautiful beads of light that peeked out from around Luna's shadow, a necklace of *Baily's Beads*. The brief flashes of light sneaked through valleys on Luna's surface. Terra saw it. Terra's children witnessed it.

Then totality happened. The sky fell dark.

Terra was upset by the eclipse. The winds kicked up. The dust drifted to coat Terra's children. Birds stopped singing. Bats flew. Coyotes howled. Ants retreated into their hills, calling it a night.

Though Corona was covered, he blanketed Luna with a 360-degree dawn on the horizon. Stars and planets winked to witness the event.

Corona said, "My darling, we only have two minutes."

"And that time is almost up," Luna said, almost in tears. "I wish I could be with you for an eternity."

"Don't worry, my love. We will see each other again next year."

"Oh, but that's too far away."

The clouds stayed away, as if sensing the brilliance of the moment. And just like that, two minutes were gone, and their perfect union began to separate. When the first light streamed through from behind Luna, Corona presented her with a diamond ring.

"Yes," she whispered.

Corona said, "Let's save Luxor for our honeymoon."

"That's three years from now."

"Goodbye is not forever. In the meantime, we'll have our annual encounters. And in Luxor, totality will be ours for six long minutes."

"Oh! That shall feel like an eternity."

***

It began as a promise six years ago. Yolanda and I received an email from Ron, asking us if we wanted to go watch the eclipse in Utah with him. I had seen partial eclipses before as a child, but this one would be the "Ring of Fire" eclipse and it would be in St. George, Utah.

Ron was a serious skywatcher. In his truck bed he had a gigantic telescope and other devices to allow us to watch our Sun. He expounded on things like annularity, umbra, and luminous bodies like the Sun, Moon, and Earth, as well as which one came in between the other two and the ratio of the perfect distance to the size of the planets. Yolanda and I only caught half of what he was saying, but we nodded and pretended we knew. Ron was really into it, and he had this feeling that somehow the Sun and the Moon talked to each other.

We arrived a day early and scouted for locations in the "sweet spot." Think *Goldilocks and the Three Bears*. One place, a campsite, was too crowded with *umbraphiles* or *shadow lovers*. In another place, the buildings were too tall and could possibly block our view. The third place was perfect. Ron said, "That's it. That's our spot." It was an eyesore with faded black and cracked asphalt, but looking at an eclipse meant looking up, so it really didn't matter.

My lips were parched. Yolanda and I walked in between rocks, scouting for shade. We passed a corner with two little boys selling what you could get for free: eclipse glasses. We joked about their entrepreneurial spirit.

The time finally came. Ron had been fussing with his equipment to get it right. And even as *first contact* between the Moon and the Sun commenced, he kept checking and moving his telescope's positioning.

The moments during the eclipse were magical. The sunlight dimmed and brought with it the wind. There was a strange sensation in the air. An eeriness to it that was both mysterious and frightening. That's what probably bothered the animals. We took turns looking through Ron's telescope at the bright red *ring of fire* around the moon. And just like that, it was over. The feeling and wonder remained. It was my first taste of catching shadows.

Before we headed out of town, Ron said, "In a few years, there will be a total eclipse." I wasn't sure what that meant. His face lit up, describing it. Once he started, he couldn't stop. I couldn't imagine something better than what we just saw. But all Yolanda and I knew was that we made a promise to be there with him. On the road back home, we threw on our cosmic playlist and jammed to tunes apropos for this out-of-the-world experience.

A few years later, Ron was diagnosed with a rare form of cancer, and he died. Yolanda and I miss him. We never said another word about going to see another eclipse.

A year before it was to happen, the news televised a story about the upcoming 2017 celestial event. I couldn't believe how fast time flew. I quickly texted Yolanda to see if she was interested, and she was. We agreed that it was something that Ron would've wanted us to do. We made travel preparations, and since Ron's equipment had been given away by his sisters, I bought binoculars powerful enough for scanning the heavens. My friend Hector constructed eclipse lens filters held together with cut-out cereal boxes to place over my binoculars. Practice was involved, even up to the evening before the event. Now I was beginning to realize the time and effort Ron put into making our viewing experience pleasurable. It was work.

We found a place in Rexburg, Idaho, and it was in the parking lot of a university, which would play an important role just before totality. The city sponsored this lot, so it was free, which was a relief to us after seeing farms touting parking for $50 or more.

The time came, and I wasn't prepared for what I was to see. Ron was in our memory. This time, right before totality hit, a university student ran up to us and yelled, "*Shadow bands!* Look at the ground!" and I did. At first, it seemed ridiculous to look down when the show was in the sky. But there were wavy lines of alternating light and dark formations, like snakes, sliding and moving in parallel along the ground. Then they vanished.

The sky went dark. The small crowd in the parking lot cheered like it was New Year's Eve. Some cried. I felt a strong emotion in my chest, and so did my friend. Just to think that we were witnessing something bigger than ourselves.

Some guy yelled, "A bat just flew by. Did you see it?"

Now that the sky was dark, the stars arrived at the party. I removed the eclipse filters from my binoculars. I managed to click one picture on my iPhone —a nearly impossible task as the binoculars started drooping from their stand. Apparently, the angle of the binoculars was too high for the stand to support. And as totality was ending, someone yelled, "Diamond ring!"

It was such an incredible experience. I can truly say that it's one of the few events for me that was life changing. We sat quietly in the car, reflecting on what we just saw, satisfied that we had kept a promise to Ron. Who knows? Maybe in some way, he experienced it along with us. But it made me feel that, with Ron, goodbye is not forever. Ron would always be with me for each eclipse.

The same was true this very week when I traveled to view another total shrouding of our Sun on April 8, 2024, in Grapevine, Texas, just outside of Dallas. Hopefully, it'll be Luxor or bust in 2027.

As I was leaving, I donned my special glasses and gazed up for one last look at the Sun and the Moon. *I wondered what they were saying to each other up there.*

Roadkill

By Aisani Washington

While driving in the blurring rain, I catch an odd shape in the corner of my eye. And because squinting does me no good, I back up to see the unfamiliar shape closely. The first question that finds me, that blurs all the others is, what would a wild animal be doing in the middle of Fairbanks—Alaska's most unfriendly city for the warm and tender— unattended? What person would just leave their animal there for the wild to consume? What kind of human at least? What lies there, cowered and cold is something I've never met in my life. The animal's fur is pulsating, so I can see that they're breathing, struggling to. And I can't take it.

I swing my car door open and push through the wind and fight towards the animal. As I get closer, the details in its fur deepen.

I have come upon a sheep.

I kneel before them and run my fingers through their fur, crusty, clamped in places, nice and overwhelmingly soft on some other parts of the body. And even through the raw smell of petrichor, I inhale the sheep's strong mammal scent. Like raw flesh that hasn't been cooked all the way. Or sweaty men on a heavy farm. My husband's a veterinarian, he'd lose it if he found out I ever abandoned a wild animal in the cold. I'd expect him to. I'd expect any human to do the same.

I heft the sheep into the back of my SUV.

When I get home, the lights are all out, which means my husband, Arnold, hasn't arrived yet. It also means I have more time to surprise him.

I help the sheep into the shed behind my home and wash them in the dark. The cracks in the shed are my only source of light until I can get to my flashlight in the kitchen. The sheep, who has the genitals of a male, has fatigued eyes. Drool taking harvest on the ends of its mouth.

It appears they've been starved before being thrown out there in the violent breathy cold. They're thinner from the stomach to the neck than the rest of their body.

It's as if he didn't eat in weeks. I turn away, look for the towel in anger with the question forming in my mind again. Why? The mother in me wants to keep the sheep. To pamper them and feed them endlessly. To defend them with my body from the evil that betrayed them. It wants them to have a home. But like any animal, their wishes and boundaries matter far more. I don't want them to be cramped by my solicitous desires.

I lay a blanket down for him to rest and leave the duties of the shed behind me.

While doing my afternoon chores, a concoction of mopping and disinfecting walls to prepare for the party my family is having here tomorrow evening, I smack on my flashlight to get a grasp on what I'm wiping down. It clicks on for three seconds. Then it's gone. I smack again. The life inside it fidgets, nothing more than a second of breath. Upstairs, as I remember batteries rested there. More importantly, I remember Arnold asking me to get rid of them because they were anti-animal, and I never got a chance to. After finding them, in the most obvious place of all—up in my room silently hidden on my work desk behind my purse—I turn the flashlight on and aim at the wall. The sheep's shadow jumps out at me. I suck in all the air in the room and grab my chest. Behind me nothing exists. There is nothing there. Just my furniture and plants. I point back at the wall and the shadow is still there.

Steeling towards the shed door outside, my hand suffocating my flashlight, my arms and shins shaking in fear, I open the shed and find the sheep lying there soundlessly asleep. The fear sticks. And the urge to find the answer thickens.

One last time, I return to my living room and point my flashlight at the white wall. The shadow is still there.

I run for my room, tripping over one stair, and running after the other before I get into my room and find refuge under my bed. I call Arnold and beg him to stay on the phone while I wait for his arrival and when he arrives, he points the flashlight himself, seeing just the emptiness of a wall. I swear to him of the shadow's existence but he just chuckles and labels me insane. And after he's gotten through with his rounds of teasing, he clenches his car keys and sighs.

"No more drinking for you."

"Arnold, I am sober, dammit. I've seen the cow."

Arnold presses his lips on my head and says, "Oh, darling. Our honeymoon was last night. Of course you were drinking."

"Pilgerflashe—Marine Style Vase from Palaikastro"
(Minoan Jar, Photo, CC BY 3.0)
By Olaf Tausch
commons.wikimedia.org/w/index.php?curid=74828607

Carpinteria

By Tyler Becker

A rose thorn, embedded under my father's cuticle

was removed too late.

His wedding ring was broken off his swollen finger

by my grandfather, careful with ancient wire-cutters,

the silver band a twisted carcass on the coffee table.

Again, slicing onions to caramelize, the sweet smell

a thick mist through the kitchen, out into the garden,

he removed a pouch of skin on his palm.

He bleeds like he speaks,

lethargically. Softly.

With sculptor's patience

my father built a sandcastle

at our favorite beach, the summer hot and stinking

of sweat and red cocktails.

The spade caught his middle finger but

we didn't notice, distracted by angry gulls and

a high tide reaching for the moat, the turrets,

the courtyard where my knights jousted,

immune to the stifling heat.

Only that night, eating cheaply on the dunes,

did my mother see the purple empty skin

where his fingernail used to be.

It frightened me, that pulpy flesh,

but he laughed as she frowned

so I laughed in turn, coveting his ease.

Our sandcastle gone with the sun,

his new ring bright in the sunset,

my mother scolded his absent mind.

Pyrite Laureate

By Karine Beltran

novice, speak:
imbibe, enchant!

sanctuary, sigh:
approach, embrace.

Each

      step

            soft poet's journey:

the pretty call of birds in spring,
an ambling summer cloud.
lovers reflect in solemn sea's devotion.

reprieve.

laureate, allay:

you

        are

        human

                enough

to unmask

           these

ill-fitting   burdens   of sex and skin

caress,   venus;

in lusty fen,

a dimpled silk,

gilded flake from angel's eye

humid bloom coaxed with sweat from brow

surpass,   Ares;

blood, circulate.

blood, boil.

body, coiled tight to bursting.

human, revile:
i hold the smoking gun

to Washington's White Temple.

      peace

      existence

      resistance

stain prim rose red
on White house lawn.

America, shame!

life lost, eyes averted.

America, shame!

If I Should Die
remember:
where you are White,

porcelain,

cold,

I am cherub-cheeked love.

I, flushed face of hope.

I, callused hands of care.

America, shame!

       Death

       forever on your delicate hands

                                     yet

       never on your sensible

       conscience.

Poppy

By Isabell Cardenas

To be a rose by any other name?

I would want it that way

To be cut and to go grey in a vase?

I'd rather be untouchable

And to be kissed by the breeze

Like a California poppy

Picture

By LuvLeighAn Clark

I use your picture to

bring my mind

happiness

I do not know

the real you

I create the person

that I think you would

be

based on your

deep grey eyes

as I envision my hands

running through

your soft hair

while watching the

moonlight dance

on the soft red

of your brown hair

I know this is just a

fantasy in my head

but in a world were

I have no connections

you are my fantasy

to reality

10:42 am, 9-6-2019

Appetite

By Kathryn Jordan

You tell me I have a great life,
invite me to dinner for my birthday.
We talk about a man who betrayed you.

What I mean is, you talk, I listen.
One more strange man at our table
as the waiter places Moroccan rice,

currants and chickpeas, endive and beets
in mustard reduction on the table before me.
Your fork lies on the blank napkin like a question.

"Not having anything," you shake your head.
We lock eyes, the same ones we said
we'd always know back when we were twenty.

I'm at a loss. How could you eat all
the bread meant to whet our appetite
while I saved room for a feast?

Star Buskers

By Kathryn Jordan

We're getting out of Dodge.
Stucco cutters and nail guns to repair
the aging house, the sense of things
falling apart. Driving out the packed 210,
through the Inland Empire, we pass strip malls
of shaved cement, asphalt, crimson neon:
Uncle Bob's Sports Bars, Jacked-Up
Gyms, Heavenly Plastic Surgeries.
Falling asleep, we drop in on a Starbucks
hiding out in a one-time Mexican restaurant
of arched windows, wide-tiled floors.
Lattes in hand, we stretch aching legs,
watch young baristas pour off the foam.
"Maybe at night this place has bands, DJs,
poetry slams." We're happy for a minute,
imagining youth building a soul hermitage.
"Let's play a gig here!" you say. "We'll tour
Starbucks all over the country for change."
"Star buskers!" I say and suddenly
we're laughing under the old tin-art stars.

The Roses Are Blooming

By Jessica Nayeli

The words "I love you" got lost in translation as they

vanished like smoke.

Your words seemed fickle coming from the tip

of your tongue.

The tongue I spoke fluent French with turned

sweet waters bitter.

I could no longer comprehend your words.

The smell of my rose perfume graces your nose.

Yet you stare at the lily across the room.

I was left alone in a world deprived of love, famished.

Bitter memories of being kissed begin to vanish.

*

The shadows of the love birds holding hands

don't haunt me.

I walk past every wrong tree.

I shield my plot from every vile serpent,

I escape unscathed.

I'm waiting, aspiring to love.

*

Apostle Paul wrote, it's better to stay lonesome,

Yet God said it's not good for man to be alone.

I'm not a man, I whisper to the wind.

My rosy cheeks and blooming chest proclaim

my femininity.

I'll befriend this season

I am no longer pretending lonely walks don't suit me.

It's pleasing the way butterflies gently dance in the wind.

*

Staying lonely brought me to the one who truly loves me.

By waiting I found true love – pure as snow fueled by fire.

Only he could shower me in grace.

Only he could cure my thirst.

My garden is flourishing.

The slate was wiped clean, my lips untouched, pure.

A quick glance, a smile, the smell of roses linger in the air.

And still I tend to my garden, it's growing, well watered.

I pluck the weeds, trim the trees,

and maintain a nourished soil.

Radiant as the sun I stand fulfilled.

Hand in hand with my creator and he sees it is good.

-   The Gardener

Absurdity of Inevitability

By Jonah Lee

The clock ticks steadily.
I sit, small and eager, in my wooden chair—
Eyes wide, waiting for the school bell's ring.

The clock ticks loudly.
I sprawl, distracted, in my plastic chair—
Watching, waiting for lunchtime's liberating ring.

The clock ticks slowly.
I slump, weary, in my aging recliner—
Counting, waiting 'till the workday's end at five.

The clock ticks no more.
I rest in the soft embrace of my bed—
Dreaming, freed from the endless waiting for chimes.

Period II Test

By Gilaine Fiezmont

I shall not lead you into temptation.
Three times seven chairs is twenty-one,
a perfect fit I'm sure
we can arrange the chairs so
your furtive looks will be fruitless,
and I shall be left
wondering
about little slips of paper
gently probing the secret
recesses of my mind.

The key could be hidden
beneath your very hand,
pale wooden labyrinth conjuring
far-away fantasies I used to have.

The room full of 3x7 minds
needs only our fever
to return to that age
when we didn't
arrange them,
colored blocks tumbling from shaky houses,
houses that grew too small
for our dimming imagination,
replaced by fingers gripping a solitary pencil.

In the room
I see a circle of light beneath a lamp,
and myself half wrapped in darkness,
unlocking archetypes, perhaps
that of Sindbad drowning in our dreams.

"Knossos, 1966"
Photograph taken in the Throne Room
by Samuel Patthey

"The Flying Dove"
(Drawing/recreation based on original
Nicholas Alan Cope Photograph)
by Yinghui Huang

From the Artist: A bird's nature is to fly, but in the original photograph by Nicholas Alan Cope it is bound by a rope. Now the rope becomes a ribbon; it's no longer a bondage but a ribbon that leads the dove to fly.

Stories, Poems, & Essays

from LACC's

24th Annual Writing Contest

Slaying Byron

By Emma Baker

Clock kicks me awake—

rain scraping the window

in the small hours.

Like a broken branch

I float down gutters

distorting through the filmy lens of memory:

your limbs long in the window,

words slick on my teeth.

Your breath hot in my midnight head.

In novels you get a measure of slack

to do irrational things with broken people.

Mad, bad, dangerous to know.

Delicious, vicious—

the smirk, the lean, the long black coat.

Dark hair, dark eyes. Chiaroscuro cheekbones.

Dark that finds your dark, makes more,

'til you can't see your hand in front of your face.

Life is a basket of fries, you told me between bites.

The world is celluloid, pulp, and plastic.

You don't have to hide from the storm anymore.

You can dance in the monsoon winds

and you will scream with joy

as lightning shoots through your bones.

But when that thunderbolt finally struck

it left no lightning at all.

I pried you off my spine

with the strength of the earth.

There are better ways

to come of age.

Yeshua & Yeast

By Rhyan Rose Kirsch

It's crazy how something so small
Can be so big.

How microbes,
Not at all visible to the naked eye,
Neither human nor pig,
How their life,
Their little microscopic life
Can change the whole of history -
How you die and who's your wife.

Bread.
Take this in remembrance of me.
Wine.
Take this in remembrance of me.

God was working in the very fabric of bacteria,

Amoebas, fungus, paramecium....

The most comes from the least.

Yeshua and Yeast.

Little Armenia

By Alina Melikian

"Shut up, dad, just shut up!"

"I put it—"

"Shut up, I tell you!"

I listened with more attention because, for the first time in this conversation, my knowledge of Armenian was enough to understand my father's yell. He seemed to forget what kind of people his parents were in almost 20 years of living on another continent. And it seemed to me that he was better able to love his parents from a seven-thousand-mile distance. Can't blame him.

"What do you have this phone for? Give it to me."

"I need it." Grandfather said without any shade of embarrassment.

"Give it to him, you … man." Grandmother appeared from the kitchen, her voice irritated and demanding. I didn't understand what she called grandpa but it probably was far from "my darling."

"I put it in the box in the garage."

My father gasped and I thought he was going to burst into cursing but he just waved his hand and left the house. A second of loud silence engulfed the room but then the angry footsteps came again, dad stormed into the house and shouted:

"If ever again you bother me with your shit, I will throw this phone and that damn money out!"

Door slammed. For the first time, grandpa showed some reaction and raised his warned glance at the door. Then he mumbled something under his breath, leaned back on the sofa, and closed his eyes.

"Do you want to eat, Ellajan?" Grandma asked.

"No, thank you, I've eaten," I said mixing Armenian with English and showing a jar of ice cream I was eating.

"Only ice cream? I've made rice."

I knew that. For the past three months, I had eaten more rice than in my entire life. Rice turned out to be my grandmother's signature dish along with fried eggplant which I hated and was successfully avoiding. But with rice, I was fed up in every sense.

"I'm not hungry. Maybe later."

"How come you're not hungry? What did you eat today?"

"I ate at school."

"Okay. I'll warm up the rice a bit later."

I grabbed the ice cream and went to my room. Grandpa was already snoring.

***

My grandparents came from Armenia three months ago. After 16 years of not seeing them (that is my entire life), I was forced to get used to what no one had prepared me for. Armenian language not mixed with English; dolma; sequence of forgotten relatives coming to greet the newcomers; black bitter coffee for breakfast, lunch, and dinner.

All these, except dolma, were annoying, awkward, and tiring. I would prefer if they moved this little Armenia somewhere to Glendale but father insisted that grandma and grandpa were old, sick, and dependent on help. Instead, they settled in the room that used to be my playroom in childhood and this, according to my parents, was supposed to satisfy everyone.

No one turned out to be satisfied. Mom was fighting with grandma for the kitchen space, dad was going crazy with his father's antics. Today he made him come home from work because he couldn't find his bag of money. And i was going crazy with all of that.

Mom walked into my room.

"How are you doing today?" she started in her "I-am-not-bothering-my-teenage-daughter-because-I-am-a-cool-mom" voice.

"Fine."

"Why are you not in the kitchen? We're setting the table for dinner."

"I don't wanna eat."

"Then maybe go and talk to tatik and papik."

"About what?"

"What's the tone? They are your family."

I bit my tongue not to say something too scandalous on this.

"And try to speak Armenian." Now I hear that more often than "How are you?"

"I speak Armenian."

"I know, sweetie, but try to speak more. It's your language."

"Are you kidding me? Mom, we are talking in English now."

"Yes, I spoiled you, but everything has its limits. You're Armenian. It's a shame not to know your native language!" her voice went severe. Now, in a mood to tell me off, her gaze locked onto an empty ice cream can.

"I see why you're not hungry. You're again eating this chemo instead of normal food. They have all the periodic table in this can!"

"It's just ice cream. They don't put anything crazy there."

"How do they make it so pink then? In my childhood, there was control over it. We couldn't imagine that there could be anything in ice cream besides milk. Soviet people knew what they ate."

"Soviet?"

"Armenia was a part of the USSR. Don't tell me you didn't know!"

I tried to get off topic, "I know. You just said it and I remembered."

I could see disapproval in mom's eyes. "Sweetie, it's your history. You have to know it."

"Mom, I have homework to do."

She shook her head disappointedly but left the room. How did they want me to care for the country that didn't even exist until grandparents came?

***

Grandpa broke his wrist on a Thursday afternoon. Dad took a day off to go to the hospital, which clearly did not make him happy. When back home he said that "he doesn't let a man work" in the voice I heard from my room and locked in his office. I put headphones on. This house got too crowded in the middle of the day.

I noticed that grandma came in only when the bed sagged under her weight.

"Go have dinner."

"I'm not that hungry yet."

"It's okay. Chop a salad for everyone. Your mother will come soon and we'll eat."

I sighed.

I was cutting a tomato when grandpa approached me. He threw a glance at the storeroom where grandma was looking for salt. He made a gesture and I followed him into the living room. I thought he needed some help with TV but instead of a remote, he handed me a 100-dollar bill.

"Thank you." I tentatively took the money. "Is it for me?

Grandpa nodded and smiled weakly. There was a black plastic bag in his hand. He nervously looked toward the kitchen, put the bag under a pillow, and lay down on the sofa with his head on the pillow. It was probably his notorious money in the bag. I felt a scratchy sensation in my chest. Looking at his glassy eyes, I wanted to give him the money back like he was a street beggar.

"Where is Hovhannes?" He asked suddenly.

"Who is Hovhannes?"

"He's not there?"

"No."

I asked mom who was Hovhannes at dinner.

"Hovhannes? You mean papik's brother?"

"I don't know. Grandpa asked where he is today."

Mom's face turned tense and serious. She glanced at dad who was bickering with grandpa.

"What's wrong? What's the matter with this Hovhannes?"

"Next time tell papik Hovhannes isn't here."

"I know he's not here. Is he supposed to come over?"

"No."

Mom's voice was so dry and brooding that I didn't insist on asking further. Is Hovhannes even alive? I turned to grandpa who was silently enduring my dad's sermons that almost crossed the line between indignation and shouting.

"What are you doing!? Take a spoon, I beg you, dad. Can you stop this?" Dad wrenched the fork out of grandpa's hands and shoved a spoon in them.

"Don't yell, please. He can hear you." Mom chipped in and then took a paper towel to clean up the scattered all over the table rice.

Grandma also tried to placate dad's anger, "Calm down. Eat. Do you want me to put a salad on for you? Ella cooked it."

I again felt that dragging pain inside. I was looking at my quiet and sad grandpa while mom was flying around him with a towel and the sensation of pitiful misery stuck in my throat as an unpleasant viscous lump. I just noticed that for these three months, he had become even more feeble and leaner than before. I shuddered. Age is brutal. It makes your son become your parent.

***

Dad kept the printer in his office as no one else in this house needed it. I had to message and call him twice to find out where the door keys were and still spent not less than 20 minutes raking through the house.

I was almost dancing in front of the laptop, adjusting printing settings. Last essay and I was done with that class. There was a blank piece of paper on the printer and I picked it up so it wouldn't get in the way of my sheets. It turned out to be not blank on the other side. I read and froze on the spot.

Surgical pathology report. But no one in my family had surgery! Clinical history and diagnosis, tissue submitted, positive for malignancy, tumor size, my grandfather's name as a patient name. It was not about surgery. Not yet, at least.

"Shit."

For a minute I was running my eyes over the paper, trying to find I didn't know what. I pulled myself away from reading only when complete silence fell in the room. The printer finished up my papers. I suddenly felt anxious guilt as if someone could break into the office at any moment and catch me doing something illegal.

I put the report back, grabbed my essay, and hastily left the room. I went to my room, sat on the bed, and didn't move for a while. "Gastric adenocarcinoma" kept rising before my eyes.

I didn't leave the room until hours later. Grandpa was asleep on the couch as usual. I stepped closer to him to hear his breath and reassure myself that he was alive. His skin tone was yellow but I didn't know if it was my imagination or not. Suddenly, he opened his eyes and sat up. Words got stuck inside me. I had never asked before if he was okay so now I felt awkward to do so.

Grandma came out of the kitchen.

"Want to eat, Ellajan?"

My grandfather went to the hospital and I never saw him again. My parents never explained anything, apparently hoping that I understood everything on my own.

I went to school, and got an A for my essay, in the theater club we put some Shakespear.

One day my mother asked me if I wanted to visit a girl in the hospital.

"Maybe some other time. I have rehearsal until 8 pm today."

"Okay, then we'll go next weekend. I also have lots of work these days."

Three days later I was told my grandfather had died.

***

Ashtarak turned out to be a dry, hot, and dusty place. Neighbor's children are looking at me while I'm running back home from the corner shop. First, I don't want my ice cream to melt; second, the way they are staring makes me uncomfortable. I don't know them but they seem to know me. I guess it is more than normal that in a town with a population of 15,000 people, everyone knows everyone.

Mom and dads went to the park they said they went to on secret dates when they were young. I, meanwhile, decided to find *that* ice cream. Mom also said that at one point dad bought her so much of that ice cream that she couldn't eat it anymore. What can be so special about this ice cream that not a single nostalgic flashback of my mother can go without it?

When they told me we were going to Armenia this summer, I was not surprised for some reason. There isn't much to sort out after grandpa's death, but I understood that. I was even a bit interested.

We live in the grandparents' flat in an old Soviet-time house that looks like it can fall apart at any moment. I climb up to the fourth floor and enter the apartment. Grandma is out grocery shopping so I can finally have my time alone after a whole week of guests and visits that started on the very day we came. Haven't ever realized my family's size is enough to establish our own village.

I open the ice cream. There is a vanilla cone inside a blue package. It actually smells like sweet milk and when I take a first bite I feel the creamy flavor from my mother's stories. The cone is soft and its texture resembles very thick waffle paper. I eat ice cream in silence, listening to the noises coming from a window that is always open because no one can close it. Either I want this peaceful tranquility or it's just because my phone is useless without WiFi. Why did I buy only one cone?

I walk towards a big cupboard. It's a whole museum piece with all its coffee cups, holiday cutlery sets and napkins, flower vases, and photos. I look at the photos for a long time. There are a lot of people in them that I don't know, but I still recognize my grandparents' faces even among the young ones. Something prickles in my chest again, as it did six months ago after his death, from the realization that the man lived in this apartment, ate, slept, raised a child, celebrated holidays, and now there is nothing. Only memories that can prove that he ever lived on this earth. Letters of a person who would refuse chemo if knew how much it cost, who didn't see his only child for decades, who is buried in a foreign land, who saw the world but didn't seem to know much about it. But what do I really know about him?

When grandma came home I said to her, "Tatik, I'm hungry."

In My Solitude

By Lindsay O'Brien

By eight o'clock in the morning, the heat already sears through Nipton like a hot knife in butter. Terri used to say it would cook the tiny metal trailer like a can of beans over a campfire, but the boys are gone now, so she doesn't say much of anything to anyone anymore.

Foxx and Mackenzie host the morning show on Terri's favorite classic rock station, 97.1 "The Point!" All she needs to get going is some coffee, a boogie, and a laugh. But this morning, no matter how much she fiddles with the dial, the station won't come through. None of them will. She takes the batteries out and pops them back in. Even the AM station that diligently reports on the traffic in the long stretches of the Mojave Desert, a voice you can rely on, is silent.

"My fault for being too far from the big city, I guess."

The coffee machine is plugged in but stays just as silent as the radio. Terri winces thinking about Ricky, how he bought the coffee machine for her, how angry he'll be when she finds out she's broken it somehow.

She is a rare species of woman, who still uses hydrogen peroxide and elbow grease to match her overgrown roots to the rest of the sallow blonde hair that falls, fried, around her shoulders. She teases it daily at the root with the same rattail comb she has used since the style was in vogue among women nearly a third of the age she is now. If it isn't broken, why fix it? The higher the hair, the closer to God. Terri wanted to be closer to anybody, even God.

A low, throbbing hum fills the space around her, and Terri fantasizes about replacing the archaic Frigidaire in the kitchenette responsible for the noise. Without a mirror, she lines her crepey eyelids with a stubby kohl pencil and makes a mental note to ask Dean about a new fridge and a new radio the next time he calls. She'll ask Ricky about the coffee machine.

"They'll call."

Terri pulls on her slacks. Her long, elegant fingernails, the same orange-y coral as always, fumble with the buttons of the starched collared shirt issued to her by Buffalo Bill's Resort and Casino. She was proud to have made the drive across the state line to Primm five days a week to deal blackjack since the boys were still in diapers, and today would be no different. There's been some talk among the dealers that the casino is pushing for electronic tables like the casinos on the Strip, but Terri takes it all with a grain of salt. Some things are just better when they stay the same. She loves the way her nails look when she is dealing the cards.

Terri has brushed her teeth but there is a strange, almost metallic taste in her mouth that lingers. She slips her tiny feet into the shoes that will allow her to stand in one spot for hours, noting from the light filtering through the windows of the trailer that it looks so much gloomier outside than the heat suggests. She thinks about an umbrella and laughs. She can't say she's ever owned one out here, where the rain brings rare and needed change to the desperate landscape.

Terri slings her cracked leather bag over her shoulder and steps out of the trailer, quickly realizing the sun and the wide expanse of sky she can witness out here in the desert are obscured by an unfathomable structure; wildly intricate and inky black – all tubes and wires and sleek paneling – a *ship*?

It is hotter outside than Terri can remember, and she has lived right here her whole life.

A beam from the bottom of the structure, the ship, cuts through the heat and reaches for Terri, bathing her in a cool light. The hum from inside the trailer, what she thought was the old Frigidaire, is clearly coming from outside the trailer, and it vibrates Terri from the inside, gently, almost with tenderness. The taste in her mouth, the taste of metal, tastes like blood.

The beam, hitting her chest, lifts her like a hand up and out of her orthopedic sneakers, up and up, higher than she's ever been, somewhere she's never gone, up and into the structure, the ship.

There is an absence of fear in Terri's heart and mind, an absence of any real thought at all. She tries to think of her boys, of their sweet faces, but she can no longer see them. She tries to think of the casino, of the radio, of the taste of coffee, but they slip away from her like she is slipping away from the earth.

"Maybe a little change is what I need."

Fast Ice

By Devin Olson

It had been cold this year, colder than this six-year-old girl could remember, and for the first time that she had ever seen, the lake behind her family's house had frozen completely over. It all happened overnight. The lake was massive, too far to see the other side, and too large to journey around safely. The girl remembered just a few days ago when she and her brother had skipped stones across the water. The sight of those stones shooting out of his hand is still fresh in her mind. She thought he was the strongest person she had ever met, and she associated his great strength with his size.

Her Brother: "Just like this, now. Ready. Pull back. RELEASE!"

A stone launched from her brother's hand. She didn't know how much older her brother was, but she knew he worked harder than their Mother and Father.

The Girl: "One day I am going to be as tall as you and then MY rocks will fly even farther than yours!"

The cold weather brought fresh work for the family who all tended to livestock. Her Mother always took care of the sheep, she called them her little "baAabies", and her Father tended to the horses better than himself. Her brother fed the chickens, but it looked more like chasing. Normally, the girl might tend to the garden, but not this time of year. The girl rarely had a moment where her family's eyes weren't constantly on her, so she took this moment to inspect the frozen lake. She grabbed her favorite pink hat and was off.

The ice seemed to come out of the rocks along the shore, creating cracked pathways towards the lake. She reached down for a smooth stone between her feet. It was jutting out of the ice and only a small knob of the stone could be grabbed. The Girl pulled and pulled until suddenly she fell back onto her butt into the cold snow and ice, stone in hand. She got up.

The Girl: "Ready. Pull back. RELEASE!"

She launched the stone with all her might, and it went quite far before clanking against the ice below. The stone slid and slid and slid until it could no longer be seen beyond a haze of fog. The girl examined closely along the ground, searching for another stone. No luck. Out of nowhere, from out on the ice, a clanking is heard coming closer to The Girl. The smooth stone she had just tossed comes sliding before her feet.

Out on the lake stood a boy about her age wearing ice skates and a pair of white mittens.

The Boy: "You won't get many out. It's fast ice."

The Girl: "What?"

The Boy: "Fast ice. It's when the ice forms around the shoreline so tight, that it holds fast to the rocks and stones. Fast ice. At least that's what my mom says."

This was the first time that The Girl had ever met The Boy, and they became the best of friends, quite quickly in fact, in a way only a child this age could. He was the one friend she had ever made, other than her Brother. For months, the lake remained frozen, and every day the Boy and Girl met on the frozen surface to skate and play. Sometimes, they would spot fish frozen in the ice, suspended in time. Other times they would spend hours building snowmen and castles. When the warm spring sun would arrive, the ice that held fast to the shore was the first to melt away, making the lake impossible to walk across. They would have to wait until the lake froze over again to see each other.

When the seasons grew warm, the lake came to life. Moose and beavers as well as wolves and rabbits who call the neighboring forest home come out to bathe and drink from the lake. Now and then a bear may have been spotted searching for salmon. But even through all this life and activity, the Girl longs for the winter, the time when she can be with her friend again. Every year the Girl counts down the days until the first winter freeze. The light hours begin to get shorter, the air grows colder, and it seems like from one day to the next the leaves go from a vibrant green to a warm yellow, until suddenly there is nothing left at all but the bare branches. The climate of the lake worked like clockwork every year, freezing over the water and bonding fast to the shoreline, and every year on the first freeze, The Girl would go out onto the lake and meet with the Boy.

During the summer the girl turned 16, her family fell on hard times. The weather became warmer this year earlier than ever before, causing crops to dry out. Food became scarce. To help make ends meet, The Girl's Brother left home to join a fishing vessel. He would send money every month, but he never came back home. Age had taken the life of the family stallion, leaving just the fruitless Mare. It was as if her Father lost his closest friend. The girl's poor Mother lost nearly all her sheep to illness weeks later. The only thing the Girl had to look forward to was meeting with her friend during the coming winter when the lake froze over.

The days went on slowly. Summer turned to Autumn and soon the leaves began to fall. The days became short and the air became cool, but something was wrong. Day after day, the girl would go down to the lake only to find the tide still flowing and the lake free of ice. More days passed and the girl remained patient, but the lake still didn't freeze. It was on the coldest day of the year that the girl packed a bag and decided to trek along the shoreline of the lake to meet The Boy. She filled her bag with dried meats and biscuits that her mother had prepared for the family, grabbed her favorite pink hat that still seemed to fit, and started off into the woods.

The cold was harsh and the air was dry, yet the lake would not freeze. Many times The Girl considered turning around, especially after catching her sweater on a tree, partially unraveling the sleeve. The loose stones along the shore slipped under the weight of her feet, clanking against each other, battering her boots and blistering her heels. But she wasn't a little girl anymore. Her body had grown taller and stronger, she had become more resilient, and the lake that once seemed so massive as a little girl now appeared so modest. Finally, after what felt like the entire day, the Girl found herself walking up to a lakeside house very similar to her own. A strange woman in tattered clothes tended to linens on the porch.

The Girl introduced herself to the woman, in a proper way her own Mother would be proud of. She learned this woman was no stranger but rather The Boy's Mother and she knew all about The Girl. Taking her into her arms, she walks with her inside and warms her by the fire, offering warm tea and fruits as well as a fresh blanket. The Girl unpacked her bag.

The Girl: "I brought biscuits, and a sausage."

His Mother: "How thoughtful. My son always said you were a kind girl. He talks about you so often. I think he cares deeply for you. He's such a sweet kid. He knew the summer was hotter than it had been in a long time and was worried the lake would never freeze over this year. He looks forward to seeing you every year, counting down the days until the winter freeze."

The Girl: "The fast ice."

His Mother: "That's right dear. Anyways, sure enough, the lake didn't freeze, so he took to carving himself a canoe out of that old tree that fell out back last winter. That young fool went out just a few hours ago across the lake to meet you at your home, in fact, he should be coming back any minute now since he certainly never found you there."

Out in the distance, gliding across the surface of the lake, a small canoe came in closer and closer to shore. It was The Boy, much taller than The Girl had remembered. His young boyish arms were now grown, paddling his canoe to shore like a stone skipping across the water. His hair caught the breeze making him look like something out of the Girl's dreams. She ran down to meet the Boy, jumping into his arms in a tight embrace.

Here

By Erika Alexandra Ramirez

In the midst of all things, I couldn't determine what my life would be like after this...

It was the middle of the night, a half-asleep Maria walked into my room, wearing her Dora the Explorer night dress while dragging her teddy bear on the floor. She asked if she could sleep in my room. I got up and walked towards her and wrapped my arms around her tiny body, carrying her into my bed. As I laid beside her, she turned to me and asked, "is mama going to come home?"

I looked at her hopeful, honey-brown eyes that had witnessed the horrors of our mother sprawled on our bathroom floor.

I had barely gotten out of school, but she was here alone.

Flashing lights were illuminating the neighborhood block, people were scattered around and passing cars would slow down to catch a glimpse of the scene.

I didn't think much of it until I saw my home surrounded by police cars and EMTs . Running straight to the front door as a policeman called out to me to not go inside, I halted when I saw Maria in the arms of my older brother, Esteban. Looking at my direction, Esteban signaled me to stand alongside him, but before I made my move, an officer stood in front of me and crouched down to place his hand on my shoulder.

"Todo estará bien," he said. I shyly nodded and looked up at my brother.

"Juli, I rushed over here as soon as I got the call," Esteban said.

"What happened?" I asked.

He sighed and the look in his eyes indicated that she won't be coming back. "Mama, will be away for a while. Once she's better, we can go see her."

I didn't want to pry any further, so I nodded 'okay.'

Three hours later, the commotion had died down and the last remaining officer got the note that my brother will be living with us for the time being.

Esteban is 26-years-old who works as a video game developer at this popular company, so he gets paid well. He told me that he'll be taking some time off to be with us.

He moved out as soon as he turned 18 and got accepted to a university in Riverside. I remember the day he received his acceptance letter; mami had opened it. You'd think as a parent, she'd be ecstatic, but that wasn't the case. She was livid. He and mami always bumped heads and I was there to watch and listen to the screaming matches unfold.

She'd tell him, "you're an ungrateful son! *¡Eres igual a tu pinche padre!*"

He'd argue back, "I'm not my father! But *no importa*, I'm leaving for school anyways. Might as well pack my shit now!"

Stomping echoed in the hallway, indicating that someone was going up the stairs, it was Esteban. I was still standing by my bedroom door and when he made it to the top, we both locked eyes. I teared up, hoping he wouldn't leave, but he turned away and went straight to his room. Within an hour, he was packed and walked out the door.

Maria and I snuggled up under my blanket that I made shift into a fort. I had lit up fake tealight candles and surrounded ourselves with our stuffed animals. She wanted me to tell her a story and I would tell her the same one I made up when she was a baby. I knew at the time she didn't understand, but she'd always request it, so maybe she did after all. It was about a star princess and her planet prince, they both are in love, but engaged to be married to other beings. In order to stop their engagements, they went to visit the Black Hole Queen who practiced the eternal cosmos and she was able to help them out with whatever they needed.

I've always enjoyed telling random stories, especially to Maria and she loves them.

She fell asleep midway during the story, just as I got to the Galaxy Ball part; moments after, so did I.

Saturday mornings would consist of me cooking some *huevo con weenie* for Maria and I while mami was nowhere. This time, we woke up to animal shaped pancakes.

Esteban called us sleepyheads and scooped Maria in his arms and placed her on her booster seat

"I decided to call off work for the week, so today we can do whatever you want."

"Ban-Ban," as my sister would call him, she never grew out of it, "let's go to Camp Noopy!"

"Camp Noopy?" He asked.

"She's talking about Knotts Berry Farm."

"Oh! Yeah, let's go there. Finish your breakfast, we'll go get ready then head out." Esteban got to washing the dishes and tidying up.

After thirty minutes, Maria and I showered together and when I got myself ready, I dressed her up afterwards.

The three of us got into his car and rode off to the amusement park.

Time went by and we arrived at Buena Park where Knotts Berry Farm is located.

If I'm being honest, it was nice not having to worry about when Maria and I will be able to eat, no caretaking, no homework; it was just my siblings and I.

The day went on perfectly. Maria rode the kiddie rides, and of course I went with her so she wasn't alone. Esteban is way too tall for the rides anyway. We ate food, funnel cake, and bought souvenirs.

On the ride back, Maria and I fell asleep and Esteban woke us up to let us know we made it home. He picked her up and went inside as I got all of our stuff from the car.

Esteban woke her up slightly so he could change her into pajamas, then laid her down and tucked her in.

I placed our stuff on the dining table and went into the living room to turn on the TV, which had Fairly Odd Parents playing.

Esteban came downstairs and sat next to me and took a big sigh, "okay, Maria is asleep in her bed."

"That's cool. Good thing about her is that she doesn't fret about going to bed," I chuckled.

"Fret? Damn, your vocabulary is great."

"It's not a big deal," I laugh.

"It is. I hated English, I was more into math and science."

"That figures, with your line of work and all."

"True. Are you doing well in school?"

"Yeah, I'm passing all of my classes. They sent me to the principal's office last week and told me they were going to tell the high school principal that I should be placed in all honor's classes."

"What? Seriously? That's great, Julia! I'm proud of you." He hugged me in a tight embrace and patted me on the back.

"Yeah, I'm looking forward to it. School is the one thing I actually enjoy."

"Damn, I was a troublemaker when I was your age. It's not like I had anyone looking after me anyways to keep me in line."

There it is, the perfect timing to ask him, "Esteban…"

"Yeah, what's up?"

"What happened to mama? Please tell me. I'm not a baby anymore."

"You're right, you deserve to know."

He continues, "Mama was never…well. It was worse before you two were born, she was barely around. Sometimes, she'd be gone for a few days and come back to leave dirty money for me so I can buy food. Then come home, not in the right state of mind. I remember her being passed out and I would carry her to the bathroom so I could wash her up. I was your age."

"She was using drugs, huh?"

"Yeah. I thought she got better after meeting your dad, but just like mine, he left you too."

"I see. Seems she never got better, because even now, she'd be gone for hours, days even."

"Seriously? It's one thing that it had happened to me, but I'm an adult now with two little sisters, it's different."

Tears started running down my cheeks and I sniffled, "taking care of Maria was hard... especially when I had to juggle it with school."

Esteban pulled me into a warm embrace and I couldn't help, but sob into his chest. Leaving tears and snot.

"I'm sorry, Julia. If I'd known, I – "

"It's okay. I understand." I glanced at Esteban and realized it's been at least two years since I saw him. He'd come by and bring stuff or check up on us, but leave again. When he'd show up, I saw him as a doting big brother; but I also saw him as the person who left us.

"But, I'm here now. Big brother is here."

For the first time, I relaxed my shoulders and unclenched my jaw. This time, it feels different. Like I knew, my big bro was here.

Poem to My Favorite Person

By Alexandra Figueroa Cuellar

Everyone asks me why I think too much all the time.

Why don't I let what I think flow?

But actually, it's because of that bad moment that

I don't want to repeat again.

That gray day,

I lay in bed embracing my loneliness,

I opened my notebook and crying I began to write,

For the first time I let my thoughts flow to the point
that only words came out.

And that immense pain I felt disappeared.

Walk slowly towards the mirror,

And gently with my hands I wipe away the tears.

I walked alone towards nowhere, and an unexpected light came out.

I looked up and saw how fast you were coming.

There were thousands of kilometers and you were getting closer,

Every step you took shortened the remaining thousand miles.

You were getting closer,

And you let me appreciate how beautiful you are,

You were turning on the light that was going out.

You carried in your hands the broken pieces that were falling on my path,

With needle and thread,

You began to sew each piece that fell,

And although it didn't turn out perfect,

You knew how to repair what you didn't break in such a short time.

You taught me that fear is just a blockage,

And "a new beginning" is like a rebirth with a new improved version.

You taught me that life tests you to make us stronger.

Thanks to you I learned to love the night,

Thanks to you I knew that I was no longer alone,

From minute one you became my life teacher,

My star, (I cried),

That star illuminates my path along with the moon.

And no matter where I am, I will always be showing my way.

A Christmas Toy

By Margaryta Ismusova

From my childhood Christmas was one of my favorite holiday. Christmas decoration is an important part of this day. I have been collecting them since childhood and each has its own story. Some stories are happy, but some have sadness. Today I tell about one of my favorite toys, which I found 26 years ago at a flea market in London.

When I was 13 years old I went on a trip to the UK and lived in London. The city made a huge impression on me with its attractions, but most of all I liked the flea markets. I could walk there for hours looking for treasures. While looking at seller's counters and store windows, one day I saw a Christmas toy hanging on a small tree in the store. There was no special beauty about her, but she seemed magical to me, "as if from a fairy tale". It was a figurine of an angel with its eyes closed and its hands raised up, as if in prayer. I went into the store and asked how much this toy cost, but it turned out that it was not for sale. I was upset because this toy I really liked and I was drawn to her for some reason. The woman behind the counter decided to tell me the story of this toy. She bought it many years ago from a family who fled Germany during World War 2. They saved a few of their things and this toy was one of them. They didn't want to sell it, but this woman was a little girl then, and just like me, she fell in love with her at first sight and then they sold it to her for 1 pound. After her story she looked at me and said that she saw the same love in my eyes and she decided to sell it to me for 1 pound and said that it would definitely bring me happiness. I was the most happy girl in the world in that moment.

Many years passed and I carefully kept this toy. Every year when decorating the Christmas tree, I hung it in the center and told everyone its story. When my daughter was born, I decided that this toy will be hers when she will grow up. And she will bring a lot of happiness to her life. But unfortunately this will not happen. When the war began in our country, we had to flee from the occupation and I remember how a German family took this toy away from the war. I also took her with me, but on the way out of the city, the military, who occupied our house shot our things and it was destroyed. Having survived one war, the toy could not make it through the second.

In my country there is a belief that if you break something, it will bring happiness. Be that as it may, she brought me joy and happiness for many years. And I often think that I can find in one day something which brings for me so much happiness.

A Female Buddhist

By Hahn Kim

Chapter 1

It was early summer. It has already been about a month since the mountains across the country were dyed red with royal azaleas. There were white hydrangeas in full bloom on both sides of the temple entrance. The shape of the flower resembled Buddha's curly hair, showing off its beauty. The road to Heungdeoksa Temple was uphill and somewhat steep. The early summer sun makes people seek shade. Jiyoung was wearing a white Hanbok—chima and jeogori[1]—, and she stopped in the middle of her steps and exhaled. She quickly took out her handkerchief and wiped the sweat on her forehead. She had her servant follow her and bring food to offer to the temple.

It was the 49th day since Jiyoung's husband passed away. She was on her way to the temple to pray to the Buddha for her dead husband. She prepared rice and fruit as an offering to the Buddha. As soon as Jiyoung arrived at the temple, she prepared white "rice bap"—steamed

---

[1] "Chima" is a Korean-style skirt for woman, and "jeogori" is a Korean-style jacket for woman.

rice—and food, and she set up a table of food to offer to the Buddha in the temple.

"Sunim"[2], everything is ready. Today is the last day of the 49-day rite ceremony, so please pray to the Buddha so that my deceased husband can go to heaven." Jiyoung said to the Buddhist monk.

"Namu Amitabha Buddha," the Buddhist monk chanted. "Madam, since your sincerity is so extreme, the spirit of your dead husband, wandering in the sky, will definitely go to heaven."

The Buddhist monk sat on a cushion and began to recite the Amitabha Sutra while tapping on the moktak, which is a wooden percussion instrument used for chanting. Jiyoung brought a Buddhist scriptures book in front of her, and she followed the monk, muttering into her mouth. She prayed that the Buddha would guide her dead husband's spirit to heaven. She also bowed to the Buddha countless times. She stood up, sat down, bent her back and bowed, then stood up again and repeated the same movements as before. Beads of sweat formed on her forehead as she bowed, repeating the same motion several times. As she bowed, her distracting thoughts disappeared from her mind.

---

[2] "Sunim" is a term used in Korea with an etiquette way in respect when people address a Buddhist monk.

"Sunim. Thank you for your hard work." She said to the Buddhist monk.

"Madam. Since you offered up the ritual ceremony every week without fail, your deceased husband's spirit must have been guided to heaven." The Buddhist monk said.

The Buddhist monk, Gwanghyun, who chanted sutras for an hour, appeared to be middle-aged, although his age could not be clearly determined by his appearance. After the Buddhist monk finished reciting Buddhist sutras, Jiyoung burned the clothes of her dead husband in the furnace under the chimney.

Chapter 2

About two months ago, Jiyoung's husband, Hyunsu departed for Gaegyeong, the capital of the Goryeo Dynasty, to take the civil service examination. In the fall of last year, 1364, he passed the first exam, the Hyangsi, and was on his way to take the second exam held in Gaegyeong this spring.

Hyunsu was able to study at "seodang"—local private village school—from the age of eight while other children at the same age helped with household chores and went out to the fields to feed the cows. Hyunsu's grandfather hoped that his grandson, Hyunsu would succeed in passing the national civil service exam. If a person passed the civil service examination, it enabled them to become an honorable high-ranking government official. His grandfather passed the civil service examination long ago and held government positions in various towns for about 20 years before returning to his hometown. However, his son was unable to study properly due to poor health and died young when he was 25 in 1350. He always looked after his grandson, Hyunsu because he expected his descendants to pass the civil service exam.

When Hyunsu was on his way to the capital, Gaegyeong, he was accompanied by a servant.

"Show your ability and do your best." Hyunsu's grandfather encouraged him.

"You must take good care of my grandson on the way to Gaegyeong," Hyunsu's grandfather said to the servant, "Take a safe route so that you don't run into bandits."

At that time, the Goryeo Dynasty was interfered with by the Yuan Dynasty, so all state functions were weakened, and the military organization was also at a weak level. The Japanese pirates took advantage of this opportunity to spread, and coastal villages on the Korean Peninsula were being plundered countless times by them. So, before Hyunsu left, his wife was worried and asked him to take care of himself out of concern.

However, one day, less than three days after leaving home, the attendant servant came home alone, covered in blood.

"Well, we were attacked by a group of thieves. I was stabbed with a sword, but I ran away quickly and luckily, I survived. However, I was unable to fight back in the face of force," said the servant.

"Where on earth were you attacked?" His grandfather said loudly.

"As the sun was setting, thieves suddenly appeared from the bushes, threatened us, and robbed us of our baggage," said the servant. "Then, my master was shouting at the bandits, but he fell down with their swords."

"I told you to take good care of my grandson before, but why did you nothing on earth?" The grandfather said angrily.

"When I approached my master and tried to protect him, one of the thieves swung his knife and injured my arm. So, I had no choice but to quickly escape." said the servant.

The servant ran into the bushes, hid, and watched the bandits. When it got dark, and the bandits disappeared, the servant approached Hyunsu. He had been stabbed with a knife, and the servant lifted Hyunsu up and put on his back. Afterwards, on the way to the village, Hyunsu lost a lot of blood. When they arrived at the village, Hyunsu passed away in less than an hour. The servant tried to take Hyunsu's dead body away, but he felt so painful on his arm cut by the knife that he could not use his arm. So, the servant set up a temporary burial near the mountain, covered it with a straw mat, and then rushed home.

Jiyoung asked her servants to prepare her coffin for her dead husband's body, and she got two workers. Then she took them and went to the place of the accident and found the body of her dead husband. She then buried her dead husband's body in the graveyard where his ancestors were buried.

Chapter 3

Since Jiyoung had got married when she was 19 years old in 1360, five years already passed. Ten years before Jiyoung got married, her husband's father was in weak health, so he suffered from a cold during the winter, and he died early from pneumonia when he was 25 years old, and Hyunsu was 8 years old. So, Hyunsu grew up under his mother's great care. Jiyoung's mother-in-law, after her husband died, expected her only son, Hyunsu, to grow up quickly, get married, and have many grandsons.

Two years after her marriage, Jiyoung fortunately gave birth to a son, as Jiyeong's mothers-in-law had hoped. Jiyoung's son was three years old when her husband died in 1365. Kyubo was too young to fully understand the fact that his father had died. When Kyubo was 8 years old, he went to "seodang" for studying. Other children there sometimes teased Kyubo, calling him a "fatherless child."

"No. My father went far away, and he would come back soon," replied Kyubo.

"You don't even know that your father is dead," the other children continued to tease.

"Mom, did my dad go somewhere far away from where he can't return home?" Kyubo asked his mother about his father's death when he returned home.

"Yes, your father has gone to heaven, so he will be fine there," Jiyoung answered.

While Kyubo was studying at "seodang," he learned about "birth, aging, illness, and death." He learned the law of the world that everyone dies when they grow old. After Kyubo found out that his father was gone, he felt very lonely. His great-grandfather loved Kyubo very well so that he would not be heartbroken. However, his great-grandfather didn't tolerate Kyubo's neglect of his studies.

At that time, Kyubo was learning "Sohak." If his great-grandfather could not hear Kyubo reading in his room early in the morning, he would quietly come to Kyubo's room and check on his movements.

His great-grandfather would ask Kyubo some questions about what he had studied and reward him if he answered well. "Sohak" was a book published in the Song Dynasty that contained the basic and essential contents of the moral norms of the Confucian society.

"Who is three helpful and three harmful friends for you?" He asked Kyubo.

"Three helpful friends for me are an honest person, a trustworthy person, and a knowledgeable person. Three harmful friends are a person who is good at flattering, a person who is different on the outside and inside, and a person who is clever with his words." Kyubo answered.

"Then, do you understand what it means?" His great-grandfather asked again.

"Of course," Kyubo answered.

"First, if I make a friend with an upright person, he will definitely point out when I have a fault. Second, if I make a friend with a trustworthy person, the friendship with me and him will grow stronger day by day based on trust. Lastly, if I make a friend with a person who has a lot of knowledge, my knowledge will expand day by day thanks to him. These are three helpful friends for me." Kyubo answered.

"Then who is three harmful friends for you?" Great-grandfather asked Kyubo.

"First, if I make a friend with a person who is good at flattering, even if I have faults, he will not point my faults out. Second, if I make a friend with a person who is different on the outside and inside, I will not be able to build trust between the two. Finally, if I have someone who is good at only talking as my friend, I will not be able to make any progress. These are three harmful friends for me." Kyubo answered.

The great-grandfather sighed in relief upon listening to Kyubo's answer.

"I want to reward you. What do you want?" He asked Kyubo.

"I have everything and lack nothing," answered Kyubo.

"But isn't there something you always want?" He asked Kyubo again.

"Then, my mother has wanted a Buddhist scripture book. Could you buy it for me?" Kyubo said.

"OK. Ask your mother what book is," he said.

At that time, the Heungguksa Temple was publishing Buddhist scriptures through woodblock printing, so he knew that her mother wanted to buy some books. Because his mother had been spending a lot of time reading

Buddhist scriptures since Kyubo's father's death, he wanted to help her.

Chapter 4

Ten years have already passed since Jiyoung's husband died in 1365. Kyubo became thirteen years old. Jiyoung's grandfather-in-law was fonder of his great-grandson, Kyubo than before after his grandson's death. However, he stayed away from his friends who he often met and drank with. Instead, he had Jiyoung prepare the drinking table and often drank alone. He felt that his life was fleeting, and he spent more time soothing his worries with alcohol than before. He naturally ate less, and his health became worse further.

At that time, the Goryeo Dynasty on the Korean Peninsula was subject to frequent invasions by foreigners. As Japanese pirates' invasions continued, epidemics frequently occurred throughout the country. Jiyoung's grandfather-in-law was in poor health, had a weakened immune system, and developed symptoms suspected of being infected with the epidemics. He had a high fever and red spots appeared all over his body. He had been bedridden for several days and could not eat well. The doctor visited the patient and examined Jiyoung's grandfather-in-law. He took the prescribed medicine but immediately poured out all the medicine he had eaten.

After that, Jiyoung's grandfather-in-law continued to suffer and finally passed into the other world in 1375. She held the funeral for him and mourned him for two years.

Chapter 5

When Kyubo was 15 years old, he grew taller, and his physique resembled that of his father. Jiyoung suddenly thought of her husband and was filled with longing. In the meantime, Kyubo grew up well without his father, but occasionally appeared heartbroken over his father's absence. He thought he would be happy if he was born as a human being and lived long and healthy. However, he had seen many things that were not like that, and he felt that everything in life was fleeting. These days, Kyubo had neglected his studies a lot. Previously, he read Confucian scriptures, and the reign of the state was one of his main interests, but suddenly he became interested in Buddhist scriptures. Moreover, after his great-grandfather passed away, he felt very lonely.

"Now, if you study a little more, you will take the civil service exam. Why are you reading Buddhist scriptures?" Jiyoung asked her son.

"Mother, if I pass the civil service exam and become successful, I can help my family. But in the end, everyone will return to dust." Kyubo said.

"My only dream is that you achieve what your father didn't do yet." Jiyoung said.

"Mother, I understand your mind," Kyubo said.

"I've been studying hard, but I keep getting distracted, so I'm going to take a break," Kyubo said.

"Then you will do that," Jiyoung said to his son.

The next day, Kyubo went to the nearby Heungguksa Temple and met a Buddhist monk.

"I am a person who is preparing for the civil service exam, but I keep getting worried. What should I do?" He asked a Buddhist monk.

"Namu Amitabha Buddha," the Buddhist monk chanted. "All living beings can forget their troubles only by taking refuge in the Buddha," he answered.

"What should people do to take refuge in Buddha?" Kyubo asked the Buddhist monk.

The Buddhist monk replied, "If you have all kinds of thoughts and concerns, please go to the Buddha, read Buddhist scriptures, and control your mind. Then, your distracting thoughts will disappear."

After being taught by a Buddhist monk, Kyubo felt lighter and soon returned home.

"Where have you been so far?" Kyubo's mother asked her son.

"I went to Heungguksa Temple and met a Buddhist monk," Kyubo answered.

"Did a Buddhist monk say good things to you?" asked Kyubo's mother.

"Yes, he said that if I read the Buddhist scriptures and controlled my mind, I would get better," answered his son Kyubo.

Jiyoung felt fortunate. Kyubo seemed to be concentrating on his studies as before. The country was not stable and continued to be in confusion. The raids by Japanese pirates became more severe than before, and epidemics plagued the people from time to time. Many people's feelings were miserable.

Chapter 6

Two years had passed since Kyubo's great-grandfather passed away. However, Kyubo was unable to concentrate his thoughts on his studies due to loneliness and distress. Not long ago, he visited the Temple, but that was the only time, and he was again tormented by all kinds of distracting thoughts.

One day, Kyubo suddenly wrote a letter to his mother and left home. His mother tried to find her son all day, but she could not find where her son had gone. When Jiyoung looked at Kyubo's desk, there was a letter on it.

The moment Jiyoung picked up his letter, her heart pounded.

"I, your poor son, would like to tell you," He began, "that your grace in raising me through all these years is higher than the sky and wider than the sea." Jiyoung continued reading the letter.

He concluded by saying, "After much thought, I have left home, so please don't look for me for a while."

To Jiyoung, this was like a thunderbolt. Jiyoung searched for her son with her household servants, but she didn't know where her son currently was. She waited for her son to come home, but he did not come back even when the seasons changed. Also, she placed "Jeongansu" water—holy water—on the pot and prayed to the gods of heaven and earth day and night that her son would be safe.

"I pray to you. I pray that the gods of heaven look down on me and take care that my son is safe."

One day, a woman who lived next door said to Jiyoung after visiting a nearby temple.

She said, "I happened to see a young Buddhist monk from afar, and I thought it was strange that he resembled your son." As soon as Jiyoung heard this, she went to Heungguksa Temple. At the temple, a "Jujaso" was built on the site, metal types were being made, and Buddhist scriptures were being published. This was a large project to print many Buddhist scriptures to help Buddhist monks study and to enable Buddhist believers to read them as well.

"Is there a new young Buddhist monk here?" Jiyoung asked the Buddhist monk there.

"No," answered the Buddhist monk. Jiyoung thought that the woman had made a mistake. Time passed again and there was no news from his son. Jiyoung's worries and worries only increased.

Chapter 7

Jiyoung was tired of waiting for her son. Her hopes for life were dashed as her husband had already passed away and her son's whereabouts were unknown. She went to Heungguksa Temple again today. She prayed to the Buddha and tried to gain peace of mind. However, when she thought about her relationship with her son, her anguish was not forgotten but only deepened.

"Cry, cry, My birds.
You are crying after waking up, My birds.
I, who have more worries than you,
also spend the day crying after waking up.
Yalliyali yalasheng yalali yala. (a repeated refrain)
One way or another, I got by during the day,

At night when there is no one to come or go,
What should I do?"
"Yalliyali yalasheng yalali yala."

She remembered a line from a traditional popular song at the time called "Cheongsanbyeolgok." This is a good portrayal of the woman's longing for her lost lovers, and it was the same as her feelings. Jiyoung's longing for her husband and her son must be like this.

Then it occurred to Jiyoung that by letting go of everything, she would be able to forget her worries. Jiyoung finally decided that she would become a "Biguni" —female Buddhist monk—and she set out. So, she went to Heungguksa Temple.

"I want to become a "Biguni" and take refuge in the Buddha," she said to the Buddhist monk.

"It is not easy to practice as a female Buddhist monk. It is very difficult to cut ties with the world. Please think again and decide it," replied the Buddhist monk.

This Buddhist monk suggested Jiyoung to think carefully about it. Jiyoung returned home dejected. If she was not accepted by the Buddhist monks at Heungguksa Temple, she had no choice but to go to an unfamiliar hermitage where Buddhist monks could not recognize her, and to become a Bodhisattva by serving food and helping with chores. Jiyoung finally visited a small hermitage.

"I am a helpless woman who lost all my parents, husband, and children," she said, "I will take care of all the chores, so just let me stay at this hermitage."

When the Buddhist monk asked if Jiyoung really had any relatives, she answered that' right. The Buddhist monk believed her answer as true and accepted her into his hermitage. Jiyoung cut off her long hair and wore a Buddhist monk's robe. She was now living the life of a bodhisattva, but she had not yet been recognized as a female Buddhist monk. At a small hermitage temple, Jiyoung got a metal type printed Buddhist sutra book published by the Jujaso and was grateful for being able to easily access the words of Buddha.

"Namu Amitabha Buddha"

Authors & Artists

Emma Baker

Emma Baker (she/her) is a poet, theater-maker, and student from Altadena. In her free time, she enjoys collecting breakable things. You can catch her other work in Kaleidoscope Magazine, JAKE the mag, and in Procrastinating Writers United's new anthology, *Long-Winded*. Follow her art on page and stage on Instagram @keepintouchemm.

Tyler Becker

Tyler Becker is a second-year English major at LACC. He was born and raised in Los Angeles and is a long-time barista. He enjoys reading poetry and fiction and has been writing as a hobby for much of his life. He is inspired by his family, their stories, and by his own personal experiences.

Karine Beltran

Karine Beltran is a tender-hearted creature native to Los Angeles, California. They spent their earliest years cultivating a love for language and a genuine belief in the revolutionary power of empathy. They have a deep respect for the artists and workers who keep their city thrumming with life. Nowadays, they are working towards a degree in the field of Child Development, with hopes of imbuing those years of passion and care into their future career.

LuvLeighAn Clark

LuvLeighAn Clark is a multi-racial (Aztec, Irish, Black) disabled artist whose journey through over 40 foster placements profoundly shaped her creative vision. As a filmmaker, writer, and painter, she weaves powerful stories that reflect on resilience, human connection, and advocacy for disabled and underrepresented voices. Her films, poetry, and art push audiences to challenge perceptions and inspire empathy, drawing on her own life's hardships and triumphs.

With over a decade in film production, LuvLeighAn is building toward a production company that amplifies fresh, diverse perspectives. Learn more on IMDb or at luvleighan.wixsite.com/goddessproductions.

Gilaine Fiezmont

Teacher, researcher, reader of international literature, Gilaine Fiezmont started writing on a dare when she was twelve. Her first immigration experience brought her from her native Switzerland to Los Angeles, California, in 1976. One could argue, though, that her first migration was a summer trip to Crete in 1965, an island she visited again and again and which occupies a special space in her heart. After spending a 'gap year' in Mexico, Gilaine returned to Los Angeles, studied linguistics, and started to work as a researcher and educator. Gilaine loves to read speculative fiction, epic fantasy, magical realism, and poems from many lands. She is exploring the worlds of web serials and independent publishing.

Alexandra Figueroa Cuellar

Alexandra Figueroa Cuellar, proudly Salvadoran, was born in 2004 in the country better known as the thumb of America "El Salvador". She has been living in Los Angeles for four years and is concluding college ESL studies in preparation for a career in Graphic Design, one of her biggest dreams. In her free time, she enjoys writing, singing or practicing her favorite sport, volleyball. Her "Poem to My Favorite Person" delighted the judges for LACC's 24th Writing Contest. Grateful and proud to be able to write and publish her winning poem, she sees it as an ideal for that person who is present at every moment of our progress and helps us get moving forward.

Sally Hawkridge

Sally Hawkridge is a writer, professional musician, and insomniac living just east of East Los Angeles with her family and other animals. When not washing her turtles, she also enjoys walking after midnight, buying musical instruments that there is no space for, rescuing spiders and lost dogs, going into long explanations that nobody asked for, and shouting at people on TV who are acting foolish.

M. Isabell Hernandez

M. Isabell Cardenas is a writer born and raised in Ventura County. She is an Aquarius, coffee enthusiast, and avid daydreamer. In addition to writing short stories and poems, she also enjoys acting/improv/clown, writing songs on her guitar and piano, and traveling wherever her Delta points can get her.

Margaryta Ismusova

Margaryta Ismusova was born on 05/28/1983 in Ukraine. From an early age, her favorite pastime was reading books and inventing stories. At the age of 7, she started writing poetry, and at 10, she participated in a young authors' competition and won first place. When her daughter was born in 2018, she started writing short fairy tales for her.

Later, they would come up with continuations for each fairy tale together. She dreams of writing and publishing a book; and hopes the dream will come true.

Kathryn Jordan

Kathryn Jordan's poems placed or won Honorable Mention this past year in the Connecticut Poetry, Steve Kowit, and Muriel Craft Bailey awards. Her work appears in *The Sun, New Ohio Review, Atlanta Review* and *Comstock Review*, among others. Kathryn loves to hike the hills, listening for bird song to translate to poems.

Hahn Kim

Hahn Kim is currently studying as a full-time student at LACC. He's from South Korea, and has lived in the Los Angeles area for three years. He was inspired to write "A Female Buddhist" when he was taking level 4 ESL. One textbook claimed that Gutenberg invented the movable metal type of print. However, the oldest metal type printed book still in existence is "Jikji," which was published in 1377 in a Buddhist temple in Korea a century earlier. So, he wanted to introduce its history by recreating the lives of people through fiction based on the historical and cultural background of the time.

Rhyan Rose Kirsch

Rhyan Rose Kirsch (he/him) is a multi-disciplined artist: actor, poet, playwright, singer, songwriter, and much more. Hailing from Sharon, Pennsylvania, Kirsch studied at Lincoln Park Performing Arts Charter School for vocal music and literary arts. In 2018, he moved to Los Angeles as a City Year Americorps volunteer, but fell in love with the City of Angels and has remained here since. He's currently in his 3rd year of studies with LACC's Theatre Academy and has performed in numerous shows, including *Kinky Boots*, *When You Comin' Back, Red Ryder?*, and *Queen of Califas*. Kirsch thanks his family, friends, and classmates for their continued support - especially his grandparents, Linda and Eric, who are the most influential figures in Kirsch's life. His professional goal is to create meaningful, educational stories for a variety of media — especially musical theatre. His personal goal is to bring joy to those around him. The most important virtues to him are honesty, curiosity, and having fun.

Igor Kholodenko

Igor Kholodenko studies at LACC.

Alina Melikian

Alina Melikian was born and raised in Russia and moved to the United States at age 18 to pursue a higher education. She studies political science, which perfectly matches her interests in history, culture, and economics. For as long as she remembers, she was drawn to writing. She wrote a first novel at the age of 9 and hasn't stopped since, and now is working to improve her writing in English. She speaks four languages and tries to use her experiences of different cultures in her creative works and hobbies.

Jessica Nayeli

Ms. Jessica Nayeli (Sanchez Olarte), author of "The Roses are Blooming", was born in Mexico City and grew up in Los Angeles, California, in a family with mixed religions (Catholic, Christian and Atheist). Due to this dynamic she denied all religions until the age of 21 when she faced a real and radical encounter with God. Inspired by her journey to faith, she writes about her experiences of life before and after becoming a follower of Christ.

Lindsay O'Brien

Lindsay O'Brien is a writer based in Los Angeles. A Las Vegas native, her fiction explores the loneliness and isolation inherent to desert living. She is currently pursuing an English degree at UCLA, and she hopes to become a teacher after graduation. This is the first time her writing has been published, and she is entirely grateful for the opportunity.

Erika A. Ramirez

Erika A. Ramirez is a 27-year-old college student who works as a cashier at a local market in downtown Los Angeles. When on her days off and not doing schoolwork, she spends time at home with her boyfriend and 2 cats, Mochi and Akira. Erika has always been fond of reading and writing, and sometimes she'll write poetry or think up new story ideas. She enjoys reading dark romances or manga and webcomics. She owns a big collection of manga and books, and often just prefers to stay home and relax in her safe little bubble.

Tvisi Ravi

Tvisi lives in the foggy hills of San Francisco with her dog and partner. After eight years working in education, tech, and consulting, she decided to revisit her passion for writing. Taking a sabbatical from her career, she now invests fully in her creative pursuits. She finds inspiration in the works of bell hooks, Kazuo Ishiguro, and Gabriel Garcia Marquez.

Liz Ogaz Ruiz

Native Angeleno Liz Ogaz Ruiz grew up reading fantasy and sci-fi on her front porch steps and attending powwows with her brother. She's a screenwriter, church pianist, caroler, Dodgers fan, has scored music for an LACC short film trailer, and makes an annual pilgrimage to Comic-Con to fuel her geek side. Among her trio of cats is Loki, named after her favorite Marvel character. She's seen two total eclipses, which inspired "Catching Shadows," illustrating that the bonds of friendship can exceed the limits of a lifetime. She thanks her parents and big brother for fueling her creative passion..

Aisani Washington

Aisani Washington, a literary fiction writer from Pennsylvania, attends Los Angeles City College as a root for his next journey before transfer. He began writing at the ripe age of eight and has not yet slowed down by any means. He plans to publish works of his own and teach English one day, but his main goal is to leave an impact on one person before he dies.

Special Thanks

Los Angeles City College Administration

Dr. Amanuel Gebru, *President*

Dr. Carmen Dones, *VP of Academic Affairs*

Mr. Joe Dominguez, *VP of Administrative Services*

Dr. Saadia Lagarde Porche, *VP of Student Services*

Ms. Vivian Alonzo, Mr. Darren Grosch, Dr. Ann Hamilton, Dr. Carol Kozeracki, Dr. Vi Ly, Ms. Angelica Ramirez, Dr. Dan Wanner: *Deans of Academic Affairs*

Mr. Juan Alvarez, Ms. Niki Dixon Harrison, Ms. Kamale Gray: *Deans of Student Services*

Dr. Anna Badalyan, *Dean of Institutional Effectiveness*

The faculty of the English & ESL Department of Los Angeles City College

Dr. Amarpal Khanna and Ms. Alexandra Wiesenfeld, Visual and Media Arts

Dr. Lisa C. Nashua, Ms. Helen Khachatryan, LACC Foundation

Made in the USA
Las Vegas, NV
06 December 2024

13431464R00105